• • •

HOW DOES IT
MAKE YOU FEEL?

· · ·

"I've learned that people will forget what you said, people will forget what you did, but people will never forget how you made them feel."

~Maya Angelou

HOW DOES IT MAKE
YOU FEEL?

• • •

Why Emotion Wins
The Battle of Brands

DARYL TRAVIS *with* HARRISON YATES

ISBN 978-0-9897103-0-5

Copyright Networlding Publishing

All Rights Reserved

www.networlding.com

WHAT'S INSIDE

● ● ●

FOREWORD

. . .

BACK IN BRANDING'S MEDIEVAL PERIOD, IN THE YEAR
2000, I published a book called *Emotional Branding*. It had the
same subtitle as this one and met with reasonable success,
probably because it was the first book ever written on the
crazy notion that brands are all about feelings rather than mere
transactions. Perhaps it was ahead of its time, but to paraphrase
the old ad slogan, "We've come a long way, baby." More and more
companies are realizing that emotions rule a brand's success or
failure—emotional equity is more important than just the facts
if we are to win friends and influence people.

Virgin fame's Sir Richard Branson kindly contributed to
that book's foreword, his words still ringing true today. Here's a
sample of his wisdom:

"The idea that a business is strictly a numbers affair has always struck me as preposterous. For one thing, I have never been particularly good at numbers, but I think I've done a reasonable job with feelings. And I'm convinced that it is feelings—and feelings alone—that account for the success of the Virgin brand in all its myriad forms.

"It is my conviction that what we call 'shareholder value' is best defined by how strongly employees and customers feel about your brand. Nothing seems more obvious to me that a product or service only becomes a brand when it is imbued with profound values that can translate into fact and feeling that employees can project and customers can embrace.

"By profound, I mean simple. Everybody appreciates being treated decently. Everybody admires honesty. Everybody believes in excellence and value. Everybody likes to have fun and to feel part of something bigger than himself.

"These values shape my rather simple view of business, but they are (or should be) universal, which is why I find it astonishing that it has taken so long to capture such a view between the covers of a business book."

Sir Richard went on to praise *Emotional Branding*, but we cannot include those remarks here because, well, this is a different book for a different era. We do, however, intend to espouse the wisdom of his determinations: that a business is always more about feelings rather than numbers if it wants to achieve maximum success. You might even say his thinking is peerless!

INTRODUCTION

* * *

THE FAMOUS ECONOMIST JOHN KENNETH GALBRAITH once said that an ordinary person wheeling a shopping cart through the aisles of a supermarket is in touch with his or her deepest emotions. He is more right than maybe he ever realized.

Next time you're at the supermarket, you can test the theory with simple observation. Watch people get lost to the world as they slowly fill their baskets. Their minds are in a whirl, doing a million conscious and unconscious calculations per second. It's easy to imagine this because you do it, too. That little voice in your head that never shuts up goes a mile a minute, as buying decisions based on old stories and new curiosities are made in consultation with the sensible and emotional systems of your brain. It is a totally absorbing, totally human process. Ultimately, after all the subliminal cogitation is said and done, it simply has to do with the way you feel about the vast array of products before you.

Strange as it may seem, many business people are just now awakening to this idea, and the simplicity of it frightens those who think business is about numbers and transactions and the price-performance ratio. Yet those who get the idea that the business of business is to create lasting relationships find new and powerful ways to prosper with the use of the "F" WORD: F-E-E-L-I-N-G-S.

This book is about the wisdom of feelings—the ability to create emotional connections with customers. It's the story of how brands use emotional connections to create customer loyalty. It explores both the mystique and experience of brands. It shows how brands with a higher purpose—those that find meaning in how they help to improve lives—build bigger profits not through altruism but through the clearly defined contribution they make to the world at large. Citing examples, this book shows how to be a leading brand, as well as a leader of brands. It elaborates on what to do and what to avoid in brand creation and brand maintenance. And this book tells the stories of great brands big and small, with insights on how those brands achieved their success.

This is not a textbook: It's a think book that adheres to the belief that serious thought is best provoked and made palatable with a bit of humor. While we have strived for depth, we have also strived for what is commonly called "an easy read." As *Megatrends* author John Naisbitt once said, "Communication and information are entertainment, and if you don't understand that, you're not going to communicate."

Above all, I want to communicate because that's what brands do.

CHAPTER 1

Portrait of a Brand Lover

● ● ●

MY FRIEND JACK IS VAIN. WHEN HE LOOKS IN THE mirror to shave every morning, I can imagine him blowing a kiss to his reflection and saying, "Thank you, God!"

Jack put off getting reading glasses for years because he thought they would spoil his image. They signified middle age and the end of his sex appeal. However, squinting began to deepen the crow's feet around his eyes, so he finally consented to an exam from an eye doctor, with all the enthusiasm of a visit to his proctologist.

A funny thing happened at the optometrist's display case. Jack discovered something that changed the way he felt about wearing glasses. He discovered the magic of a brand: Giorgio Armani.

When he first tried on Armani's elegant spectacle frames, he decided that, far from being a handicap, they added a certain *je ne sais quoi* to his noble profile. Wearing them was like playing dress-up with his face. He could see, in a certain light, he wasn't stretching the truth too far to say they made him look like Gregory Peck in the classic movie *To Kill a Mockingbird.*

The Armani's did the opposite of making Jack feel like a four-eyed geek. While they indeed appeared to give him the look of a Gregory Peck, he, as a fan of old Italian movies, changed his mind and decided they made him feel like the debonair Marcello Mastroianni nonchalantly accepting an encounter with the young, nubile Sophia Loren as they were in their steamy old films. Today this couple might be the equivalent of Brad Pitt and Angelina Jolie, but the idea is that the right stimulus can sometimes make a fantasy appear very real.

Jack went a step further. When the very attractive, young salesperson told him the glasses looked just right for him, he decided that she could very easily be the Sophia/Angelina of his dreamlike buying state.

Jack's Armani's were certainly among the most expensive frames in the display case, but out of the dozens of options for sale, he could see no other choice. He plunked down his Visa card and ordered three pairs: one for reading at the office, one for reading at home, and one for distance and watching TV. A couple of thousand dollars later, with his Armani's carefully ensconced in their handsome designer cases, Jack was a happy man. Although he had bought the glasses from a shop in a mall, the Armani brand made him feel as though he had made his purchase at the designer's store at 6 Place Vendôme in the 1st arrondissement of Paris, where, with his enhanced sophistication and Angelina on his arm—sorry, Brad—Jack could saunter across the street for a glass of Bourgogne Chardonnay at the bar of the Ritz. Jack, being an old movie buff, would imagine Ernest Hemingway and F. Scott Fitzgerald sitting at the bar, casting admiring glances both at his choice of companion and his stylish eyewear.

If you think this is an exaggeration, you know neither Jack's imagination nor a brand's power to enhance personal identity. Of course, Jack didn't spend half an hour indulging his fantasies; in fact, he probably spent only a few seconds constructing this brand drama, but that is the way great brands work. They come to us in the subconscious, seconds before we make the buying decision. Jack's dreamlike state, while he was in the optometrist's shop, was very much like the supermarket experience: As you look at the magnitude and multitude of colorful options, you are absorbed in making flash decisions that involve feelings about what will taste good, clean the best, or be healthful for your family.

Whether you are buying Armani glasses or a particular brand of orange juice, the principle is the same: You are using a four-letter word that starts with *F* to make yourself emotionally secure. That word is *feel*—how your customers feel about your brand in comparison with others isn't a casual question: It is the *crucial* question.

The importance of feelings isn't exclusive to the marketing and sales department: Chief executives and their financial counterparts also have a vital interest. It is the job of everybody in your company to court people like Jack with feelings that turn him into a loyal convert for your brand. That is why the most important question you might ever ask is the title of this book: How does it make you feel?

The fact is that we develop a deeper emotional response to the brands in our lives than our rational minds can fathom. While our emotional response is not always logical or rational, it is, above all, human.

Jack's glasses are, in fact, a few bits of ground glass and plastic held together by small screws. And, very likely, Armani's production costs are comparable to the cheapest glasses in the display case. They don't work any better than the others to improve Jack's vision, Jack could have chosen frames that were a fourth of the cost, *and* Giorgio Armani probably doesn't even manufacture them. However, none of that matters in the bright light of Jack's perception.

There's an ugly kind of logic dictating that Jack is a sucker for buying into a bunch of fashion hype. As is often the case, logic would miss the point, and we can only thank heaven that not everything we humans do is logical.

The value of the new glasses exists in Jack's head and heart. The value to Jack is how they make him feel. A brand's power is measured by how it makes you feel. You might say you have justified reasons for choosing one brand over another, but even these reasons translate into emotional preference. They simply help us rationalize emotional choices to ourselves and, just as important, to others. We often hate to admit it, but emotions rule the roost we call the mind. We humans acquired this habit many hundreds of thousands of years ago, and it never went away.

If you scoff at this idea, think about the car you drive. Is it simply a means to get you from A to B? Is there no emotion in your draw toward a brand? And how would you feel switching to one you might deem inferior? Why does the water you pay for taste better? And why on earth would we pay nearly as much for a bottle of Evian water as we pay for a bottle of beer? Tell the guy sporting a Harley-Davidson tattoo that Honda makes a more macho bike. If you know somebody who owns a Rolex, suggest that he would be just as happy with a Timex. If a banana could decide its destiny, would it rather be a plain banana or a proud Chiquita? Ask yourself why a gift that comes in a Tiffany Blue Box shows such a special appreciation for the recipient. If these aren't emotionally driven questions of intrigue, we don't know what they are.

On a totally mundane, almost absurd level, ask why a huge majority of people prefer Morton Salt—even after it's explained that salt is salt; no difference exists between brands; less-expensive brands are identical products; you can't make premium salts; and no matter how you slice it, one molecule of sodium combines with one molecule of chlorine to make sodium chloride. Salt is a commodity, but, amazingly, Morton Salt is overwhelmingly preferred. The truth is when you buy Morton's, you buy a healthy pinch of trust along with your sodium chloride—trust that the product is clean and uncontaminated, a fair measure, and the same product your mother, aunts, and grandmothers used for generations of successful cooking.

Good old Morton Salt is full of emotions you simply do not find in other brands of salt. This explains its 50 percent market share. It's a wonder that any other salt brands continue to exist. Maybe I am as much the proverbial sucker that Jack is with his Armani glasses, because I will never toss any other brand of salt into my shopping basket!

It's no exaggeration to state that one brand of salt that is probably no different from any other has staked a claim to my emotions without my conscious thought. Only when I think about it now does the package's slogan "When It Rains, It Pours" come to me as a familiar story from childhood—the illustration of the little girl under her umbrella makes the brand even more compelling. I would urge that the Morton people never change or update it. When it comes to salt, old-fashioned is good fashion. I think it was Yogi Berra who said, "Nostalgia isn't what it used to be"—but when it comes to Morton Salt, Yogi got it wrong!

Going back to luxury, it's plain to see that Giorgio Armani designs beautiful glasses, but Armani's name and the link with expensive, exquisite taste imparts the magic that had Jack nearly changing his name to Alessandro and going around talking in a romantic Italian accent. He knew of the Armani name long before he had ever thought of buying glasses, and he vaguely associated Armani with the finest Italian style and elegance. The effect was that, when Jack was confronted with the brand at the exact time he was about to make a purchase, the name Armani spelled out a reputation for the best of the fashionable best. The Armani magic, cultivated over many years, was ready to pounce on Jack's imagination at the precise moment he was faced with a buying decision.

The emotion engendered by the Armani name shows that a product is made in a factory, but both the value and the brand are in your head and heart. Nothing in business is more obvious than this fact: Products leave factories by the thousands every day, but brands are sold one at a time, and they are sold with F-E-E-L-I-N-G-S in mind.

What can happen next is that Jack's enthusiasm will act as a missionary for the Armani brand. Everybody he knows is going to be treated to the sight of him in his new specs. Jack will post his photo on Facebook for several hundred friends to see—and those friends will be enticed to try the brand. And Jack doesn't call them "my glasses": He calls them "my Armani's." He'll elaborate on buying a couple of Armani suits, shoes, cologne, and a wristwatch. In a few years, when he needs a brand-new lens prescription filled, it's likely he will want to at least try on the latest Armani frames ahead of all other marquee fashion brands. Consequently, the loyalty he now *feels* for the Armani brand could be worth many thousands of dollars in the years to come. You could even say that Jack has become a walking pyramid scheme for the Armani brand. However, if the Armani brand, through negligence or oversight, lets Jack's fervent brand loyalty fall through the cracks—as, so far, his response from the brand has been limited to this single transaction—Jack is likely to lose his passion for the Armani brand. Along the road, he could be tempted by another brand, and an opportunity to cross-sell will have been lost, perhaps forever. In the new age of one-to-one marketing, this could be a very costly shame.

The potential of a powerful brand to generate sales at higher prices is awesome. It doesn't matter the product made or service offered, be it old, new, big, small, real, or intangible. The customer might be a man or a woman. Maybe you are in a business-to-business situation. You might be a hospital or a steel company, a scrap-iron yard or a dairy farmer, a software IPO or a packaged-goods giant, but whatever you are, you have every right to the higher profit a brand can generate. Brands don't have any sense of the difference between consumers and business-to-business customers: A brand is an equal-opportunity employer.

This book will show you how to have a brand that stands out from the crowd, with as much ability to create passion in your users as Giorgio Armani does in Jack.

That's a promise.

Incidentally, I sometimes take perverse pleasure in cooling Jack's jets. When he came to me fishing for compliments about his new Armani's, I looked him over for a minute before I said, "Very nice, Jack. They make you look like Alan Greenspan."

CHAPTER 2

What You Are in for: The Six Brand Imperatives

● ● ●

NO MATTER WHAT STAGE YOU FIND YOURSELF IN approaching the noble and profitable destination of becoming a great brand, it's worth looking at what the really good guys do.

In my work with brand leaders, I notice they have very little reluctance to share what they do and how they do it. It's as though they want everybody to get in on the act of becoming an effective brand. In the long run, the more trust people have in brands, the easier the work becomes for all brands.

Through Brandtrust, the company I founded in the late 1990s to help other companies become better at better branding, I have worked with many execs who already get it and just as many who have no idea what all the fuss is about but think they should find out. Business education does not include much reference to the fact that branding is not really about facts at all; instead, it's about emotional attachments and the lifelong pursuit of identity. A successful Harvard-MBA Information-Technology leader actually told me the "mumbo-jumbo" of marketing had left him brain-dead. I explained that he obviously wasn't brain-dead, but he might be brand-dead! He laughed and said, "Okay, so you explain it to me, and I'll buy lunch."

This is a request I both love and hate. It means I get to share what I have learned over many years as a brand advisor—I tend to do so with considerable passion—but it also means I have to explain something soft and emotional that is out of the context of most business discussions, and I am expected to do it in 15 minutes! Additionally, a brilliant mind who can teach me a thing or two about electrical engineering and technology might well think my preoccupation with such things as the emotions of his wife's shopping habits is frivolous. But those emotions are what branding is all about, and to get the conversation going, I usually start with what we at Brandtrust call "The Six Brand Imperatives."

1. Brands are about feelings, not facts.

Above all, people make decisions about you from the way you make them feel. You are what people feel about you, not what you project. For example, if a person who wants to convince you that he is a really nice guy simply says, "Hi. I am a really nice person," you might think he is conceited, egotistical, or self-delusional (and "nice" is certainly not the word you would use as a response). However, suppose he's very late for your meeting; sweaty and distressed, he bursts into the office and says, "Really, really sorry I'm so late, but an elderly lady got hit by my cab, so I had to take her to the hospital emergency room, and I waited until she got to see a doctor and had an X-ray, and luckily she is not really hurt and…"—well, you get the picture. You are suddenly understanding of his tardiness, and if you sense honesty in him, you are likely to believe his niceness to be sincere. He can declare his niceness over and over, but it won't ring true until you *feel* it's true.

Products and services are in the same boat. In fact, we are better off thinking of products and services as the jumble of emotions people feel about them. The purpose of a car is to get you from A to B, but we give it much more responsibility than simple function—some people even name their cars. Jack loves his sporty VW Golf GTI and calls it "Tigger." When I asked him why, he said it wasn't big enough to be a regular tiger but it was a "ferocious wannabe." Jack actually likes his car because of what he thinks it says about him *to other drivers*, it conveys that he knows performance but doesn't want to be thought of as trendy, and he anthropomorphizes it with a distinct personality. You probably do something similar with your wheels. No matter what category a brand fits into—anything from a disposable diaper to a mink coat, a college education, or a downtown condo—you never buy without ascribing some kind of emotional value to your purchase. People say they "love" their iPhones. They "adore" their new red Zappos shoes. They "can't live without" their MacBook Pro. Ferrero Rocher chocolates are "to die for."

When I say brands are about feelings, not facts, I'm proposing once again that people make buying decisions based on how their purchases make them feel. Does the brand make them feel more confident, secure, cool, pretty, smart, savvy, or happy? Does it represent their values? Would their friends approve? What do their choices say about them as people?

Without these questions, there would be no need for more than one brand of anything. There are people who think human consumption has gone too far, that the proliferation of stuff has plainly gone mad, but to think this way denies the fact that human beings put a very high price on identity. In *The Social Contract*, Robert Ardrey states that a man's three basic motivations are to seek stimulation, security, and identity. I would certainly ascribe our quest for identity as pretty high on the list of what makes us tick. Brands are a form of self-expression and one of the major ways we keep score.

One of our people at Brandtrust, Kristian Aloma, is going for a PhD on this very subject. In a paper he wrote, "Narrative Identity and Luxury Products," he puts forth the idea that a brand tells a story of not only who you are but who you want to be. Throughout your life, you grow, weed, and nurture your identity. Your identity is not a thing; it is a story, and there are brands—symbolic representations—which serve as props in your life. They bring tangibility to the story and keep it moving forward.

For example, the objects in our homes are more than nuts and bolts, fabric and stitching, functional and practical: They are vehicles of your identity, part of you. They furnish the personal theatrical stage in your life's daily drama. They are symbols of who you are, such as the guy who drives a minivan to prove he is a good father. The French philosopher, scientific thinker, and mathematician René Descartes said, "I think, therefore I am." Kristian Aloma's research suggests, "We are what we have." And Jack says, "We are what we want and can't have. That must mean I am a Bentley GT."

Looking at how brands affect our unconscious thoughts and feelings provides refreshing insights for all marketers who want to better understand what makes you, me, and the rest of the world tick, not just for profit but for the sheer fun of getting to know customers as human beings. We are not Affluent Singles or (my favorite horror) DINKS (Double Income No Kids). These artificial designations, known as "segmentations," are created to make marketing seem easier, but segments pigeonhole us into amorphous masses that simply do not align with the way we think of ourselves, our families, or our friends and neighbors.

"Empty Nesters" is a funny example of what seems like a convenient marketing-shortcut segment that takes us down the wrong path. Insurance companies like to portray the golden years of retirement as getting the kids out of the house, through college, and launched into careers so that good old Mom and Dad might have the advantage of cutting down on expenses and go sailing in their 40-foot yacht or taking a long-wished-for African safari. Empty nesting might also signal the unattractive prospect of a future life of lonely dinners at home or the unpleasant prospect of declining health in a not-too-distant old age. Empty nesting could be delightful one day and dreadful the next. One company we know of even coined the term "Post-menopausal Empty Nesters." Can you imagine people thinking of themselves in such a way? Doing so is objectionable, misleading, and insulting—hardly a good way to approach a prospective customer. Stop using words like "target market" (a target is something you hit), and replace it with "audience," "customers," or even "the elderly."

Sorry, folks, but people do not play these cluster games. At Brandtrust, we are often called upon to dig below segmentation data, get at the deeper emotional drivers that are similar in all consumers—what we call "human universals"—and give a more accurate and actionable picture. We help our clients understand that the real world does not exist so they can sell stuff to target groups. Reality is about the daily drama you and I live.

American-Canadian journalist Jane Jacobs, an expert on city life and author of the influential book *The Death and Life of Great American Cities*, once said that watching life go by on her Greenwich Village Street was like attending a kind of ballet. I sometimes remember this when I walk on a busy

Chicago street in the company of strangers going about their daily business in the same way that I am. I can see that they are contained as though in a deep secret by the whirl that is going on inside their heads. Absorbed in personal fascinations, it's a wonder people hear the stop-and-go traffic and the taxis' honking horns. They appear oblivious to their surroundings: buildings, traffic lights, shop windows, and even other people. I can only guess their mysteries are not found in stories told on CNN or geographies or philosophies but in the deeply personal foibles and fables of family and friends, work and play, loves and hatreds, harmonies and discords, comforts and discomforts, joys and disappointments.

In the old film *Zorba the Greek*, Zorba (played by Anthony Quinn) was asked if he was married. His answer, accompanied by a huge grin and then an exuberant solo Greek dance, is one that has stuck with me as a lovely lesson in common humanity: "Am I married, you ask? Yes, I am married ... wife, house, children—the whole catastrophe!"

In the context of a life—witness to doubt, certainty, sadness, and happiness—it might seem trivial to discuss a brand's role in these engrossing privacies. But we must look beyond doubt and certainty and within the happiness and sadness because those emotions are where brand stories must truly reside. Further, when troubleshooting the attraction of our sainted product to these extremely distracted people, we have to think about its contribution to their enchanting dramas, its implementation within their deeply personal sense of identity, how it eases, improves, and adds happiness to the journey of their life's journey – or somehow makes it more fulfilling. When we master these things, we create the magic of a brand. The process is simultaneously simple and complicated but a very exciting ride.

2. Branding is the most powerful yet most misunderstood business strategy.

We are still learning why people are drawn to some brands and not to others, but it seems glaringly obvious that a brand's presentation has a lot to do with the way people feel. When a brand is not true to what it promises, you know it. You feel it more than you think it. Why should the way we personify brands be any different? Think about one of your preferred brands. Does it care enough about you to perform as promised? Does it speak to you with conviction, not conveying phoniness? Would you ask it out on a date? Would you take it home to your mother? Would you buy it for your best friend? Does it smell and feel good to your touch? Is it literally good enough to eat? Does it manifest affection? Is it worthy of your adoption? If somebody offered to buy it for more than it's worth, would you take the money and run?

Your demands on a brand depend on the life stage of your personal story. For example, a high-school teenager's idea of fashion will most likely change as he or she reaches the age of 30 and is gainfully employed (at least we hope so). Our stories change with time; our needs and desires change with the chronology of identity. Not many people go skiing at the age of 80, so they are unlikely to be in the market for the season's hottest ski fashions. Jack is a bit of an anomaly because most people his age do not fly off to Buenos Aires to take tango lessons, which is exactly what he did to escape the cold winter. Becoming a parent changes much of your destiny, as does marriage, embarking on a career, etc. While demographics are not nearly as important as we used to think, the stages of our lives are not totally absent from the appeal of one brand over another. Whether you are nine or 90, all brands have one thing in common: If they break their promise, you are likely to forever banish them from your life. Additionally, since nowadays you have a powerful voice through social media, brands that disappoint you will undoubtedly suffer the same fate with all of your Facebook friends.

A company's internal considerations also count for a great deal. We know of bosses who view their employees as commodities. These employers also do not grasp the simple notion that an unhappy employee will not be an effective brand representative out there in the world where it counts to display good manners and simple kindnesses to customers. If you do not care about your people, why should they care about you?

Acclaimed business advisor Peter Drucker once said we have to assume relationship responsibility as a duty. I have heard of medical schools that are just getting around to teaching bedside manners, which I assume has something to do with the revolutionary idea that a good doctor takes the time to sympathetically listen to a patient's problems. You have to wonder why this needs to be taught, but in the crazy-busy world of a hospital, time is scarce and sympathy can suffer. This is very important to the brand of medicine a doctor practices. In *Blink*, Malcolm Gladwell states that busy and inattentive doctors who rush through a diagnosis and make a mistake are more likely to be sued for medical malpractice. However, doctors who listen carefully but still make a mistake rarely get sued! Does this sound like familiar consumer behavior when it comes to our brands?

Lenience is granted for brands that are striving to do the right thing for customers while apathetic brands get fired and, in some cases, even sued. Once again, it boils down to the way we feel. A brand's onus, in everything it does, is to make us feel that the brand is authentic and worthwhile.

As stated earlier, business schools do not teach the emotional side of branding, which is a poor state of affairs, simply because, in both the short and long run, a brand is nothing more than how people feel about it. Many an MBA grad gets his or her coveted degree without a basic understanding of the brand's role in people's lives. This kind of critical insight is ignored at a brand's peril and to those whose success depends on a future in marketing. Being good at crunching numbers and assembling and analyzing data are skills worth acquiring, but these skills are useless if you do not prioritize branding's emotional side and its connection with customers.

Do you remember the once-popular song, "Little Things Mean a Lot"? It would make a good anthem for companies out there that do not understand a consciousness of doing what you say you will do when you say you will do it, a vital part of what works for a brand. By the way, drilling your employees to say "Have a nice day" does not constitute customer appreciation, but while a lot better than a scowl, it is an automaton cliché. It is manners by rote, when a simple "Thank you very much" might do the trick. I heard a refreshing sign-off by a BBC news anchor the other day, which made me think that he avoided the usual anchor's farewell when he said, "Thanks for having me." It struck me as both original and genuine when he also said it with a beaming smile. If I go to a restaurant and the staff knows the menu in detail, tempts me with visionary descriptions of dessert options, and (when I'm leaving) gives me a cheery wave and an invitation to "come back soon," I think of these important personal touches, but they are often absent elements when it comes to dining out.

It's what you might think of as "soft-side differentiation." I was recently in Toronto on business and had to send an early-morning FedEx package. At 7 a.m. I called the FedEx office and said I had to send a rush package to Chicago. The person on the other end said, quite spontaneously, "Oh, goodie! We love doing that kind of stuff!" It was as though I were maybe the third person to ever call on FedEx to deliver a package. That young man's simple utterance made my day.

As usual, Jack has an unusual take: "I can't think of anything more obvious than practicing customer care by actually caring. It goes back to the biblical idea about doing unto others as you would have them do unto you. This advice has been around for 2,000 years, and it comes from a guy who knew a thing or two about leading with values."

Mark Twain (Samuel Clemens, if you prefer) told us to "Always do right. This will gratify some people and astonish the rest." There is nothing like a pleasant surprise to endear a customer to a brand.

3. The brand is not part of the business. It is the business.

Once you realize a brand becomes a living emotional entity in customers' minds, you understand that a brand is more than a collection of utilitarian parts or services designed to put money on a financial statement. People do not distinguish between what and who you are. More and more, a brand is what your customers make of you rather than what you might plan to have them think of you. In today's age of one-to-one marketing, customers have a lot more to do with what and who a brand is.

You might be very proud of the fact that your wonderful product performs better or does the same job for less, but your customers' assessment is what ultimately counts. Your customers now create the value, which exists only as an emotion, a wee spark of recognition worth only as much as it does or does not contribute to a customer's identity. This is rarely something they think about. We have found that people don't invest a lot of time in the details. Parity prevails, and good performance is merely the price of entry. Once they become aware of a brand's existence, people construct a short, simple mental note of what it means to them. That is all you get and is really all you need. If the mental note strikes a deep enough initial chord, the brand can be recalled time and time again without any effort. It simply finds a tiny place in one of the creases of your gray matter to become a kind of reflex. With the plethora of choice available to us, it's a good thing we do not have to agonize over every brand we put in the shopping basket that is our mind.

Other customers help us keep tabs on our chosen brands—of course we can communicate our experiences to them—but unless there is a dramatic change in a brand's performance or attitude, or if something new and exciting comes along, our usual brands just keep on sailing along without our taking much heed, e.g., Samsung's new boat-rocking Android phone system that some people swear works better than the Apple iPhone. That, combined with perceived flaws in the latest iPhone 5, caused a few hearts to nervously flutter at Apple, a perfect illustration of how a stellar brand must remain witty. As with the proverbial latest and greatest, there is always a new star waiting impatiently just offstage. When it comes to people's feelings about their brands, nothing can be taken for granted, including the kind of fanatic loyalty Apple seems to inspire. As the American poet Emily Dickinson wrote:

"Fame is a bee.
It has a song–
It has a sting–
Ah, too, it has a wing."

Brands have a wing, too. Of the 50 original companies that made up the Dow Jones Industrial Average, only General Electric remains.

By now, I hope you are getting the idea of what a brand is, but it's also important to know what it is not. A real definition is slippery because it's as hard to define as what makes you

you, and you would not restrict a reference to yourself with the facts alone: that you are many strands of double-helix DNA suspended in a large volume of H_2O!

By the same token, a brand is not your factory, machinery, inventory, patent, logo, or advertising. It is not even really a product for one very simple reason: A product is made in a factory while a brand is made in a mind. Most important, it is the job of everybody, from the receptionist to the members of the board, to understand they are all equal-opportunity attractors. They, too, are the brand just as much as the product or service is.

4. The little things you do are more important than the big things you say.

You may profess to have great customer care, but if I make a call to your company and get a rude or apathetic response, you are mud. You do not walk the talk. You are a lip-service outfit, and, metaphorically speaking, I might just put you to the sword.

If, on the other hand, I get a cheery response from a happy person eager to listen, that person deserves a place among the better angels of those who keep their promises. This is not hard to figure out. It's the same as engaging customers face-to-face. Whether I go to a store, book a flight, place restaurant reservations, or conduct any other type of personal brand business, it is not unreasonable of me to expect simple courtesy. We have all encountered horror-show service we can recall and recount in full detail for all to hear, and it is so unnecessary. I still get fumed about my run-in with the people at Northwest Airlines *more than 10 years ago.* I never went back to them, and now I'll never have to because the brand no longer exists. (Hmm. I wonder why.) Brand leaders have to remember the obvious: The customer has options and will exercise them freely.

Of course, just the way a good friend can get away with an occasional lapse, so can a respected brand. Customers are not totally unforgiving when it comes to slip-ups by favored brands they are accustomed to. If you are a Ford lover, a manufacturer's recall might annoy you, but if it is made in a timely manner and properly framed in good conscience, it is not such a big deal. There may still be a Ford in your future.

Many years ago, the prompt, forthright, forceful way Tylenol faced a product-tampering scare was a classic lesson in crisis management. The company moved quickly to remove all products from retail shelves and worked diligently to advise the public about the potential threat. The way it was handled and its prompt conclusion created more faithful customers than the brand had before the event. A tumble off the quality wall doesn't always require "all the king's horses and all the king's men" to put the brand back together again.

However, in spite of all that positive emotional equity in the bank, even the Tylenol brand can crumble when it forgets that brands need to do the right thing. A more recent recall of Children's Tylenol led people to charge that the brand was too slow to respond to the problem, drew the scrutiny and reprimands of the FDA, cost millions in sales, and severely damaged the brand's reputation with consumers.

It is a tragic tale when you run across a brand that seems always in a bad or uncaring mood. I avoid department stores because I often feel abandoned in a retail wilderness. I give bad reviews to all who will listen about a restaurant that serves up good food with bad manners. Like most frequent flyers, I dread the announcement "Overbooked." I avoid the bank teller who chews and snaps gum in my face. You get the picture. This kind of experience will not make me feel good about your brand and never induce me to become a loyal customer.

I have a hard time imagining managing a brand with any other intent than winning customers the way we win friends. Would you invite me to your home but make me wait at the front door until you got around to answering it? Would you fail to take my coat or leave me sitting in the living room by myself for half an hour? Would you serve me a warm beer with a hair in it? Would you leave me sitting by myself at the dining room table while you got on the phone to talk to your cousin in Oshkosh? If this sounds like a gruesome picture, compare it to the way some brands appear to operate.

The financial department of a large national charitable organization decided to eliminate the cost of return mail sent to thank donors for making contributions. This truly great organization, right-minded and caring in its everyday mission, simply lost its way by trying too hard to be efficient and cost-effective. It's good to cut expenses, but financial executives rarely ask, "Is there a cost in reducing this cost? Is there an emotional cost to our actions? How will our customers feel if we do this?" Fortunately, the charity soon realized the error and corrected it. Donors feel appreciated and personally involved in the good work when the organization makes the effort to thank them for their generosity. Getting this right also led to a substantial increase in subsequent giving that more than covered the cost of thank-you notes.

A brand that works according to a shared mission, an ideal that every employee can understand and get behind, is the best and most effective way I know to improve behavioral performance. This may seem obvious for service businesses, but it's equally true for product makers. If you manufacture a product and enlist everybody in a shared mission of improving customers' lives, you set a standard that all can get behind and feel part of. This includes such things as encouraging line workers to suggest improvements to the manufacturing process and rewarding them for acceptance. It's conveying that employees do not work for the boss: They work for the customer. They work for the people who pay the bills and in many cases leave the tips.

In the job of meeting a customer's needs, amazing things happen when you enlist the help of every employee. The Japanese learned a great lesson from the eminent management guru Peter Drucker (a most prescient business writer), who taught them that the endgame of a business is to make customers long before the business makes money. In his book *The Principles of Management*, Drucker expands on this idea:

"Making money is a necessity of survival. It is also the result of performance and a measurement of it, but making money is in itself not a performance. The purpose of a business is to create a customer and to satisfy a customer. That is performance and that is what the business is being paid for. The job and function of management as the leader, decision maker, and value setter of the organization, and, indeed, the purpose and rationale of the organization altogether is to make human beings productive so that the skills, expectations, and beliefs of the individual lead to achievement in joint performance."

This basic truth of business raised a few eyebrows in its day. Even now I get amazed reactions when I pass on this fraction of Drucker's wisdom to some very savvy business leaders who see the bottom line as the one and only Holy Grail, but nothing makes more sense than shared understanding of shared purpose as the way to achieve success. Today's most powerful brands never take this for granted. We will be looking at many examples of how their lessons were well learned. The word *company* finds its roots in the word *companion*, and it means "the sharing of bread." If by this we mean mutual emotional, as well as physical, sustenance for employees and customers alike, it is a lovely word indeed.

5. Every brand is a story. How will yours be told?

Storytelling is the most elemental form of human communication. It started when our species was still living in caves. Hunters sat around the fire, roasting mastodons and spreading rumors of their outstanding bravery, no doubt exaggerated, during the excitement of the hunt. These stories are the source of our most enduring myths; indeed, the ancient Greeks used myth to explain natural phenomena and eventually as the inspiration for their spiritual nurture. With a little updating, myths have never stopped being swapped and retold house to house and tribe to tribe, even today. It's no coincidence Nike is the Greek goddess of victory, as well as the name of a popular sports shoe. Additionally, when you see Mr. Clean's bald head and physical splendor, does he not resemble Hercules, the divine hero who cleaned Augean stables?

Gossip is a story with a social force for both good and bad. When you listen to the daily news on TV, you are hearing a kind of gossip with social value. People are always on the lookout for an audience they can share their experience with, and you will be comforted to know the things that could resonate with your brand. However, depending on what they say, you could also be dismayed. People talk about brands because their choices say a lot about who they are and who they want the world to think they are. In many ways, brands become a kind of language or shorthand. Unless a brand is boring, it will engage people. Very happy customers might even volunteer to be brand ambassadors; there are new technologies to broadcast their endorsements more effectively person to person than the best TV commercial ever written. That's because, as you will hear repeatedly throughout this book, there is no more powerful medium than gossip, word of mouth.

This is the way to make sense of the fact that Facebook now has half a billion people around the world spending an average of 40 minutes a day "talking." Add to this other chat outlets like the now-ubiquitous Twitter, with half a billion users recruited in its short life and another 135,000 signing up every day for a total (so far) of 91,000 tweets per second. Then add again 100 million bloggers, 2 billion Internet users, and more than 4 billion mobile phones mostly all ringing at the same time.

You get the idea that the customer is king, not to mention queen and taskmaster and judge and jury presiding over the fate of the brand that is your pride and joy. I recently read that 1.8 trillion gigabytes of data were generated in 2012. Considering the Internet has been around only since the early 1960s and did not become commonly used very much before the 1980s, this is a staggering number to contemplate! Folks, we more than likely ain't seen nothin' yet!

The old Buick line "Ask the man who owns one" turns out to be prophetic in the annals of marketing because the idea of telling your brand story on a one-way street via conventional media is now gone. What's also deader than a dodo bird is the old idea that minds are out there waiting to be stuffed with what you say about your brand in your TV commercials. It was never true in the first place, but many marketers behaved as though it was. Major advertisers often appealed to the lowest common denominator and seemed to put everybody in that class. Ad man David Ogilvy felt compelled to admonish advertisers with the advice, "The consumer is not stupid. She's your wife." Perhaps this would not be classified as politically correct in today's parlance, but during advertising agencies' creative revolution led by the genius of Bill Bernbach, it rang a few bells. His legendary Doyle Dane Bernbach agency in New York was the advertising revolution's principal spawning ground.

Our very own Jack was part of it all and, at least in his own mind, still is. Bernbach's merry band and its offspring were on a mission to end what he calls "the age of phoniness in advertising." Their kind of advertising ushered in a new species of ad that was refreshingly candid, simple, disarming, human, and beautifully designed for the ultimate in clarity, involvement, and relevance to people's lives. "It worked," Jack said, "because every ad was a story that took people by surprise, by not taking itself too seriously. It even made virtues out of what could be perceived as negatives, so people gave it credit for honesty. It told us 'Avis is only No. 2 in rent-a-cars. We try harder.' Frank Perdue Chicken told us 'It takes a tough man to make a tender chicken.' Heinz demonstrated the difficulty of getting its ketchup out of the bottle because it's 'Just too thick, too rich to run.' While Detroit was giving its cars impossibly fanciful names and *still* does, the 1960s revolutionaries and their brave clients had the guts to call a car The Beetle, and when it came out with its first automatic transmission, one of the ad headlines I wrote said,

'You call us ugly. Now you can call us shiftless.' Levy's bread made the most of its heritage by telling New Yorkers, 'You don't have to be Jewish to love Levy's.'"

These ways of talking to customers do sound like stories. They were legendary in their time, but the operative word is *legend*. Jack defines advertising as "having a bit of a chat with the customers." Having a conversation with people was a breath of fresh air in a day when we still saw silly white knights on white horses charging across the TV screen, not in a funny Monty Python kind of spoof but with the serious intent to impart that "New Ajax laundry detergent is stronger than dirt." The ubiquitous use of the word *new* always made me wonder if the brand had been pulling the wool over everybody's eyes before it was "new and improved"! Now, even worse, everything is "all-new" and comes with the tautology of a "free" gift.

Until quite recently, packaged-goods advertising mostly relied on formulaic, slice-of-life scenarios that involved two women talking with the stilted dialogue of stereotypical housewives culturally tied to life in a suburban kitchen. One woman showing another how the brand could come to the rescue of a domestic problem with a sure-fire solution was constantly portrayed in these awful little dramas. Brand people used to defend these commercials with testimony to their effectiveness, but American viewers can all heave a sigh of relief that such inanity is less prevalent during our evening entertainment. In fact, today's leading packaged-goods brands now take a decidedly higher road, as we shall see in a future chapter.

Jack shares his formative Doyle Dane Bernbach experience:

> "We didn't talk about branding in the way we do today. A brand was simply a thing. The ad campaigns we created gave products distinctive personalities, as a means of cutting them out of the herd. It was through advertising alone that we did what we nowadays call branding. I don't think companies thought about it much more than that. What we now call branding was the ad agency's job. The client's job was to make and sell stuff and stick it to the competition."

Advertising is still most effective when it follows Jack's prescription of treating people as humans rather than as marketing targets, but I bet you can flip through any magazine or click through an evening of TV to find no more than a few ads that are worth your time, which makes Jack very upset because it is a worse sin than being annoying. Why is there so much "bandwagon cool" (as Jack calls it)? As one example, he invites anybody who will venture to go through *Harper's Bazaar* or *Vogue* with him to see if they can find a single fashion model who doesn't look as though her puppy just died—or who looks as if she is glaring mad-as-can-be at you, as though you just insulted her grandmother. And why, he asks rhetorically, does every male model have the *de rigueur* look as though he has a three-day growth of beard? Jack's point is that ad stories often lose their potential effectiveness because they simply melt into sameness.

In contrast, the Burberry brand tells us stories with its choice of models, costumes, and props in brand-appropriate scenarios reminiscent of the way we use clothing to define ourselves to ourselves and others. The ads are what we might think of as organic to the brand, which is the quality all effective brands aim for when they use advertising to tell their stories.

Conventional media faces a changing future. Magazine readership has gone through a massive decline. I recently read that, from only one year earlier, single-copy sales of U.S. consumer magazines fell 8.2 percent in the second half of 2012. Old standbys like *Newsweek* and *Time* have converted to online publishing. Martha Stewart is giving up publishing in favor of merchandising. With the advent of the Internet, you no longer have to blacken your fingers to get "all the news that's fit to print." In *The New York Times*, there are new ways of broadcasting that are sure to change how we get our favorite TV programming (more about this later). As many of you already know, rather than being chained to a network schedule, today's media entities, like Netflix, provide convenient on-demand programming. Meanwhile, conventional broadcasting is still very much alive and stickier than we thought it would be 10 years ago, and audience behavior has so far not changed very much at all.

As reported in *The New York Times*, BTIG researcher Richard Greenfield says viewing declined in 2012, for the first time, but people are still watching television five hours a day. For marketers, this means we continue to get our brand info from TV, radio, and print. Conventional media is still a major impetus behind the fact that, in the next year, Americans will spend $6 trillion on consumer goods and services. Though Greenfield says YouTube is where cable was in 1986, he does not think it will take 30 years to overthrow TV.

However (and it is a *big* however), even 10 years ago, the one-way brand stories that were the norm now get a lot of help, and sometimes hindrance, from the two-way chat that people can swap back and forth in a simple text message. Because everything they buy is branded in one way or another, people are excited about and even enjoy discussing their purchases by name, for good or bad. Marketing campaigns must now combine conventional and digital media in ways that cover all bases of customer interaction. Perhaps we have to start thinking that everything a business does is media. According to Lee Clow, TBWA/Worldwide Global Director of Media Arts, "The best ad for Apple ever is the Apple Store." If you have ever been in one, you discover not only an illuminating retail experience but a formidable example of how employees and product design can be the foundation of the relationships that drive business growth. So, yes, everything is media.

Whether you realize it or not, with the daily mass absorption of multisourced information, your brand is a story more and more in the hands of your customers, which means you have to listen to them with greater care. If you listen hard enough to what they think, feel, and do, they can help you make your story the one that stands out in the formidable mess of media clutter.

By telling of Jack's youthful adventures in the advertising business, I do not mean to imply television commercials are necessarily brand stories. Intrinsic brand stories have deeper roots than selling propositions. Heinz ketchup, for example, probably exists in your mind with a deeper meaning than thick, rich red stuff that takes a lot of coaxing to come out of its bottle. That's certainly one image. Seeing it in a commercial might trigger distant memory flashes of how good it was on your mother's meat loaf or how much fun it was as a child to smear a golden French fry with gooey red stuff and how it stuck to your fingers, which made it fun to lick off. In other words, the brand story is more than a product attribute; in fact, it is not stretching things too far to say all great brands broadcast inherent mythic qualities born of lifelong habits, familiarities, and memories we mostly take for granted.

Jack says Heinz baked beans heated in a pan on a gas stove and piled on thick, buttered toast trigger a distant memory from his childhood in Scotland when his grandfather came to his house for lunch before taking him to the launching of the great ocean liner *RMS Queen Elizabeth* at the docks in Glasgow. He remembers, at the age of about three, this was his first encounter with canned baked beans. They were the most delicious thing he had ever tasted, made even more so by the attention of his doting grandfather, who had helped build the iconic ship and made him feel terribly important by taking him to its launch with the celebratory crash of a champagne bottle he thinks he can still hear on its noble hull. With powerful images, sensations, and associations stored in memory beyond our conscious control, this is how our brand myths are born and retained in our heads.

Jack still loves his baked beans on toast, and as an essential part of this treat, he still sees these childhood images. He made me laugh when he added that his most ancient memory is of his mother telling him if he played with his belly button, his bum would fall off. He says, "I am still careful with it; I retain the visual fear of having to go through life without my rear end!" Such is the way our personal myths are born. As novelist Saul Bellow said, "Memory keeps the wolf of insignificance from the door." Former Nike and Starbucks exec Scott Bedbury taught us this valuable lesson:

"A great brand is a story that is never completely told. A brand is a metaphorical story that's evolving all the time. This connects with something very deep—a fundamental human appreciation of a mythology. People have always needed to make sense of things at a higher level. We all want to think we are part of something bigger than ourselves. Companies that invoke that sensibility invoke something very powerful."

What a wonderfully poetic way to express the idea of brand as a story! Later, we will hear from many such business artists in hopes they will inspire you to avoid Shakespeare's theory that life "is a tale / Told by an idiot, full of sound and fury, / Signifying nothing."

6. Brand Ideals: The importance of standing for something important.

All of the great brand builders seem to know a fabulous secret that presides over every brand's ultimate fortunes. They realize a truly important and effective way to connect deeply with people is to attach a brand to a fundamental human value. They discovered centering brands on ways they improve people's lives is paramount to a brand's ultimate success.

Truly successful brands go beyond the old idea of utilitarian advantage, what we used to call the Unique Selling Proposition. Their marketing mission is to communicate an enduring, timeless higher purpose not just in what they say but in everything they do. Former Procter & Gamble exec Jim Stengel writes about this in his book *Grow: How Ideals Power Growth and Profit at the World's Greatest Companies.* As the title suggests, he makes it very clear that communicating brand ideals is not a frill: It is not altruism. Rather, he links a brand's impact on society to much higher profit. It may sound cynical to say ideals make the cash register ring, but linking the two makes ultimate sense to employees, customers, investors, and all other stakeholders. By defining a brand's meaning in the public good, we find the ultimate persuasion.

For example, I have long admired IBM as a company with the best business leaders I know and as a company of *integrity* and *authenticity*, these two words most effectively drawing people to a great brand. The critical insight is this: You cannot hide from who and what you truly are. What you stand for is not opaque. We sense the real you long before we bring it to consciousness. It's as though a brand has body language and facial expressions that communicate in primitive ways we all subconsciously understand. Enduring ideals cannot be faked. We can smell a sham a mile way, and IBM is no sham.

Big Blue's big mission is to show us how technology can improve the world. Its chosen and succinctly stated purpose is to "help people make a smarter planet." When I read or hear this, I believe it because it resonates. I admire it and am touched by it. I feel confidence in IBM and would feel in good company if I decided to do business with them. When I see real employees in their TV ads saying, "I'm an IBM'er. Let's build a smarter planet," I do not feel as though I am on the receiving end of a pitch: I feel as though I am dealing with people who are excited about their lives and ideals and want to share them with me.

The real deal is IBM people practice what they preach. Their stated purpose has helped them develop a business focus that endures the volatility of markets and the changing face of technologies, as indicated in an insightful IBM ad:

> "Until recently, marketers saw consumers only as vague demographic blots. So it's no wonder so much marketing missed its audience, or bored it, or annoyed it. A new generation of CMOs, however, is applying new analytical rigor to vast pools of transactional and social data. This allows them to develop deeper profiles of individuals, and to design marketing that is more

relevant, more personal and, ultimately, more like a *service* than ever before."

This statement shows that, even in its advertising, this company decidedly takes the high road. The single vision of making a smarter planet is now IBM's North Star that unifies the endeavors of more than 400,000 employees scattered across 170 countries. It can be said that IBM people are the IBM brand because one formidably powerful purpose welds every one of them together in their $100-billion Fortune 500 Company.

When I think about IBM, I wonder how employees must feel about going to work there every day, knowing a hugely important concept presides over their every move. This concept is not marketing hype but something much bigger than the usual promise brands make to their customers – and it can remain hugely important as long as IBM's employees do their part in keeping it alive, by never forgetting its meaning, by living it and breathing its inspiration every day. It's not hard to imagine that a singular, well-stated vision makes every individual feel he or she is the real brand leader, that the real boss is not a person but the common purpose of the brand ideal. I can only assume that IBM employees feel as though they are working for a lot more than a paycheck and that their contribution is going to count for more than an end-of-year bonus. IBM proves the theory that employees make a difference when they believe they make a difference.

British retailer Marks & Spencer promotes more than the goods it has for sale, partnering with Oxfam in a program called "shwopping," where for every item a customer buys, the customer is encouraged to take something from the closet to recycle. It sounds like a crazy thing for a retailer to do, because, for example, you might decide to keep your old duds rather than buy new ones. However, the brand hope is every store will take back one garment for every one it sells, and it is done in the name of sustainability. The brand undoubtedly does this to create good opinions, but as a major UK brand, M&S is betting that its customers will realize it is more than lip service.

Drug giant Merck will tell you it is "in the business of preserving and improving human life. All of our actions must be measured by our success in achieving this goal." The money is where the mouth is when you see the work done to cure river blindness along the Amazon, as well as work done to help eliminate tuberculosis when it turned into an epidemic in Japan after World War II. They were not profitable ventures, but what do they tell you about Merck's vision of social responsibility? How much appeal does it have when it comes to recruiting dedicated scientists? The Roman Empire's mission was to spread civilization, and the still-standing bridges that Romans built more than 2,000 years ago are a testament to the power of its inspiration.

Compare these examples with one large company's mission that said, "Our mission is to enhance the asset base of the owners." Pin that on the wall, and see how many yawns you get. And how about the sentiments expressed by one prominent marketing exec who said, "The sole purpose of marketing is to get more people to buy more of your product, more often, for more money"? I'm sure the employees loved the motivational power in that one.

This is the kind of thinking that might go down well at a stockholders meeting, as they love that macho stuff, but it bears no resemblance to the real world of what brands must do to create and keep customers. It's dead thinking from an age of marketing to masses rather than to individuals. It's thinking that looks inward at what might be ideal for the company rather than for the customer. For companies like IBM, it's brand blasphemy of a very tall order that is a thing of the distant past.

Of course, companies have to make money, and, of course, making money is necessary for growth and investment, paying wages and utility bills, and keeping the wolves and the taxman at bay. In other words, if there's no margin, there's no mission. But that's as obvious as saying you can't breathe without oxygen. As Sherlock said to Watson, "It's elementary." A company cannot survive without creating a surplus for all kinds of reasons, including the attention of investors. Growth is as desirable and necessary for a company as it is for an individual, and growth requires financial and intellectual resources. The facts, dreams, and ambitions of our lives often need money to come to fruition and do not stand still in the quest for identity. Nobody scoffs at a healthy year-end bottom line, least of all Merck or M&S (I can't speak for the Roman Empire), but I also know profit starts and stops with engaged employees attracting engaged customers, without whom there is no bottom line to count! Today we even see brands putting off immediate profit for years, as they perfect their performance for payoff down the road. This reminds me of a quote from Charles Kettering, American inventor, and head of research at General Motors: "I am vitally interested in the future because the future is where I will spend the rest of my life." A huge brand like Facebook is still trying to figure out how to make more than a half-decent profit. I sometimes think Facebook runs on faith alone.

Thinking the only thing that matters is how much cash is added to the bottom line, people forget that between making and selling a product, something rather important has to happen: The product somehow has to make an appearance in your head. You may write the words cornflakes on a grocery list, but I bet you simultaneously visualize your brand's packaging so that you are ready to just pop the Cornflakes box in your shopping cart when you get to the store. You might change your mind, which often happens, when you are standing in front of the dizzying cereal display, but without the occurrence of that process, you can't sell anything from Coca-Cola to Jockey shorts. To get on people's grocery list, you first have to be on their minds. An idea, a feeling, or an image has to appear, even if it is only for a millisecond, when a need occurs, and that flash is the job and the obsession of marketing.

Buried somewhere in my adventure with buying Band-Aids this morning is an example of how the flash works. The little voice in my head turned the process into something as seemingly momentous as admitting there were no weapons of mass destruction in Iraq. For one thing, standing in front of the display case is a daunting prospect for somebody in a hurry. Then the little internal voice kicks in:

"Who knew there were so many choices? It's like Band-Aids have become a commodity like Kleenex. And should I get cloth or plastic? I thought Elastoplast only made big bandage stuff to cover a knee or a whole head or something. And what kind of brand is Option? Is it the house brand because it's a few cents cheaper? It's probably as good as the others, but, hey, you can't go wrong with good old Band-Aids. I can hear the jingle and see the cute kids singing it: 'I am stuck on Band Aid brand 'cause Band Aid's stuck on me.' If I had any guts, I'd get the cartoon ones. There's nothing like a Fred Flintstone Band-Aid to make a boo-boo feel all-better. Hey, get a life, Travis. Get the 50-count plastic Band-Aids, and *gedoudaheah*, as they say in Noo Yawk."

I don't know how long this little internal dialogue took, maybe no more than a second or two, but it sounds to me like feelings are hard at work here. If you are thinking that perhaps I don't seem to have a lot to do, I can see a genius like Albert Einstein, who was busy figuring out the universe, having to go through the same process. It probably didn't take more than a few seconds, but it shows how a brand can come to the rescue in moments of confusion or indecision. The familiar came to the rescue in the great Band-Aid drama. I went with what I know and trust and what my mother used to stick on me. This is why marketing a product or service is about creating relationships much more than it is about creating transactions.

Logically and chronologically, like a horse before a cart, the relationship always has to come first. And I hope it will be as lasting as a good marriage so that our esteemed and worthy customers stay with us happily ever after. The ideal objective is not that customers buy one bottle of Coke but that they buy several every week *forever*. As any astute marketer knows, the largest percent of sales from a big brand, like Coke, comes from a much smaller percentage of customers. This proves we must look after the customers we already have, in addition to chasing new ones. It's also true that whatever brand experiences created your best customers are the same experiences that will create more customers.

When lunch with my delightful and very bright inquisitor came to an end, he sat quietly for a while before he said, very simply, "Wow. Thank you. That's a ton of stuff to think about."

I hope the journey of this book leaves you with the same pronouncement.

CHAPTER 3

How We Think We Think and How We Really Think

* * *

LET ME TAKE YOU THROUGH ANOTHER PERSONAL scenario: When I got up this morning, I went from the bathroom to the kitchen, where I opened the fridge, took out the juice, set it on the counter, opened the cabinet, grabbed a glass, and set it next to the juice. I got the Starbucks coffee out of the freezer, pulled the carafe from the coffee brewer, put it under the faucet, turned on the water, spun around, opened the cabinet behind me, and reached to retrieve the coffee filter from the top shelf. By the time I got the filter positioned in the brewer and scooped the coffee, the perfect amount of water was in the carafe. In one fluid move, I shut off the tap, poured the water in the brewer, slipped the carafe in place, and pushed the start button. Total time from bed to brew? Five minutes or less. Total amount of conscious thought about what I was doing? Zero. In fact when I was doing all of this, the little loquacious voice in my head was reminding me I had a 10 a.m. meeting, and I had to pick up the dry cleaning, make an appointment to get a haircut, and, well, you get the picture. I literally had nothing to do with any of it, except that I was there performing as instinctively as a trained monkey.

Without giving it any more thought than I do, you go through similar morning rituals, and it proves something quite important. Most of the time our minds and bodies work according to the admonition in the Nike slogan: We "Just Do It." It is a blessing that disguises itself without explanation, and it has great importance in the way we perceive and respond to brands.

If you had to think about scratching your nose or looking left and right at a traffic light or tying your shoelaces or any of the automatic things you do every minute of every day, you would not be able to function. Our brains are designed for the advantage of quick thinking. There's not much time to cogitate when a saber-toothed tiger is licking its chops as it sizes you up for the possibility of a tasty lunch. You don't have to tell your feet to do their stuff. Fight or flight takes over, and you do not have to reason that running for your life or throwing large rocks is a lot safer than thinking about it. Taking time to reason with a hungry tiger is just not rational. It has been this way since Homo sapiens was a pup. Our lack of conscious thought about human action is quite stunning. This includes very large issues, like why we build fences, form nations, go to the moon, fight wars, fall in love, are inordinately fond of our children through interminable childhoods, seek status, and even choose one brand over another.

We have learned a lot about human consciousness without truly understanding the organ from which it emanates. We have sent men and women to the moon, even plotted the formidable human genome system, but we could only have performed these incredible feats because we had the necessary technology. No tools yet exist to even remotely explain what goes on automatically in our enigmatic gray matter. This vast gap of knowledge is the reason behind the brain-research initiative proposed by President Barack Obama in his State of the Union address.

Neuroscience now estimates that the circuitry of the brain has 100 billion neurons interacting with 10,000 other neurons to produce up to 1,000 trillion connections. If you can grasp those jaw-dropping numbers, you are a better, much calmer person than I am. The proposed research project could cost more than $3 billion over the next decade. While we have yet to decipher its many benefits, it will undoubtedly be worth every penny. As a recent *New York Times* headline read: "The next frontier is inside the brain." Could our explorations turn up cures for mental illness, addictions, and other strange compulsions? Just think what it would mean if we could learn how to curb aggression. It makes landing a man on Mars feel like technical puffery.

One of nature's great mysteries is why we have such poor insight into our innate behavior. Apparently, the human brain was not designed to understand itself. With enough intelligence to invent everything in the world, from the wheel to space travel, we haven't the slightest understanding of what makes us repeatedly commit the kind of incalculable horrors we see today in the news. Even a cursory glance at history turns up comparable genius in the ways we in the Western world have also learned to inflict pain, suffering, and death. No nationality is immune. No religion is above reproach. No government is without the ability to lead us into uncharted moral waters. As the Western world basks in the relative comfort of civilized societies, we do not have to look very far back to recall the slaughter and other unspeakable atrocities associated with world wars. These abilities are just as much a part of our nature as those we beckon from the angels. As we talk about the allure of brands, let us not forget the pronouncement of philosopher Thomas Hobbes: "Life is solitary, poor, nasty, brutish and short," which are still the watchwords for those who live with the eternal pessimism of ever-present stagnant societies with no hope of liberation from war, hunger, and the oppression of ghastly regimes.

I have occasionally been accused of having a utopian outlook when I talk about branding and human nature, but I am by no means blind to the presence of devils in our midst. Charlatans, demagogues, power merchants, thieves, and Machiavellian jerks are not beyond my notice. I could exhaust the English language further with derisive comments on the scandalously reckless and reprehensible behavior of some of the banks we wrongly assumed to be above reproach. One commentator recently gave us the ultimate irony when he pronounced our banks are now too big to jail!

However, I also have faith in our evolutionary heritage as social animals with a need to cooperate for the sake of survival. With all the available technologies, we think we might have become very different from the generations of our grandfathers who measured their hours in the slow, silent eons of agriculture, but are we really very different? Traditional human nature still works pretty well today. Maybe we have to accept the bad along with the good. People are not made to be perfect, but we do what we can. When I discussed these things with Jack, he gave me a paragraph written by his old boss, Bill Bernbach: "It took millions of years for man's instincts to develop. It will take millions more for them to even vary. It is fashionable to talk about *changing* man. A communicator must be concerned with *un*changing man, with his obsessive drive to survive, to be admired, to succeed, to love, to take care of his own."

We are forced by a kind of blindness to live with our mysteries, and we somehow manage to get along without understanding them. As Freud saw, we are oblivious to our deepest motivations, but in ways that are more chronic (even in some cases more grotesque) than he imagined. In a recent *National Post* article, evolutionary psychologist Hank Davis adds to this thought by reminding us that our brains are still stuck in the Pleistocene era and cautions us: "Our problem is not with the cognitive mechanisms that we have inherited; it is with our inability to turn them off. They work too well and too frequently."

Our brains, it would appear, work mostly on automatic pilot. They live in a dark, mysterious place behind a locked door we conveniently ignore because they need no conscious help to get along just fine. We have to remember that in comparison with time's eons, we are still infants. Molten lava became home to 5 billion species 4 billion years ago. One single cell was formed 3.5 billion years ago. A 3-inch-long water worm appeared 550 million years ago; and 99 percent of all species that have ever lived are now extinct. Dinosaurs lasted 165 million years. Tools are 2 million years old, and we did not come along as Homo sapiens until 200,000 years ago. I got these numbers from Jack, who says, "Putting it that way, we have to give ourselves a break for just getting around to figuring out the miracle of what we are doing when we write a grocery list." I can only hope he didn't make the numbers up to impress me.

We do, of course, think and reason. All we do is not reactionary impulse. Right now I am even thinking about thinking. You can't do quadratic equations or memorize irregular French verbs without using your noggin. You can't find an address in a strange city by osmosis. Writing a coherent sentence takes mental agility, as does solving crossword puzzles and persuading Lady Luck to let you win at *Texas Hold 'em*. Along with trying to understand life's mysteries, we have our ability to reason, which is second to none in the animal kingdom and a very useful resource. Luckily, the emotional and logical systems of our brains are quite willing to cooperate, and neuroscience has come a long way to explain how it happens.

Antonio Demasio, one of the foremost neuroscientists in the world, shares his breakthrough research in his book *The Feeling of What Happens*:

> "For example, work from my laboratory has shown that emotion is integral to the process of reasoning and decision making, for worse and for better. This may sound a bit counterintuitive, at first, but there is evidence to support it. The findings come from the study of several individuals who were entirely rational in the way they ran their lives up to the time when, as a result of neurological damage in specific sites of their brains, they lost a certain class of emotions and in a momentous parallel development, lost their ability to make rational decisions."

In his book *How Customers Think: Emotional Insights Into the Mind of the Market*, author Gerald Zaltman informs us about the reality of how people process information:

"In actuality consumers have far less access to their own mental activities than marketers give them credit for. Ninety-five percent of thinking takes place in our unconscious minds—that wonderful, if messy, stew of memories, emotions, thoughts, and other cognitive processes we are not aware of or that we can't articulate... Rather than actually guiding or controlling behavior, consciousness seems to make sense of behavior after it is executed."

Apparently, we don't have nearly as much control of our thoughts as we think we do, suggesting we should change the way we think about how people think.

Harvard psychology professor Helen Langer gives an obvious but scarcely realized insight that makes for valuable, personal psychological fodder. She says if we do not think about our thoughts, we aren't likely to improve them. We can do so simply by being more mindful of them. According to Langer, it's a "subtle change in thinking, although not difficult to make once we realize how stuck we are in culture, language, and mode of thought that limit our potential."

In one study, Langer showed how elderly men improved their hearing, memory, and dexterity by consciously thinking and living as if they were actually in a younger stage of their lives. Apparently, we are what we think. We just don't spend enough time assessing or managing our thoughts. I've learned it is impossible for others to dictate our feelings unless we allow them to—your mind is your very own sovereign territory. Next time you say "So-and-so really makes me mad," try to realize he only makes you mad with your permission to do so. When you alter your thinking, your thoughts change, too.

Malcolm Gladwell, one of my favorite authors on the subject of thought process, takes thinking out of esoteric theory and shows us its practicalities. In his book *Blink: The Power of Thinking Without Thinking*, he explains our mind's everyday operation. He shows us not only how instinct is actually a very reliable source of decision-making but also how it can lead us astray, and we are more effective when our thinking is led by conscious thought. All of you marketers who want to better understand how people make blink-of-an-eye decisions, before you're even aware of it, put *Blink* on the forefront of the must-read list.

According to Gladwell, most of our decisions are made through rapid cognition and a process known as "thin-slicing," which is our nonconscious minds finding patterns in situations and behavior based on very narrow slices of experience. He says, "Thin-slicing is not an exotic gift. It is a central part of what it means to be human. We thin-slice whenever we meet a new person or have to make sense of something very quickly, or encounter a novel situation."

Thin-slicing helps us cope with the complexities of life; otherwise, life is just too chaotic for us to manage all of its details and preserve our sanity. An encounter with the aforementioned saber-toothed tiger is a good example, but it does not have to be that dramatic. We evaluate a brand by thin-slicing before we consciously think about it. It is the way we recognize thought patterns and make snap judgments. For example, we first see and perceive a color several hundred milliseconds before we can think or say, "Red light." Our foot seeks the brake pedal long before we think to act. Our nonconscious minds do the job with signals that automatically tell us what to do.

We also see people and decide very quickly what we think about them. Gladwell exemplifies actor Tom Hanks, who is impossible not to like. We don't know Tom from Adam, but

I bet no matter what role he plays in a film, you immediately sense him to be a decent, trustworthy, funny, and a down-to-earth man you would be glad to see marry your daughter! That's who and what he is, and we sense it without any effort. That is the Tom Hanks brand if you will. It's what Tom Hanks "feels" like, and with this example in mind, you can easily see how thin-slicing helps us come to "think" about brands with the same kind of instant but informal judgment. (We might even thin-slice our initial attraction to potential life mates, which can work for or against us if we choose to ignore the theory that haste can indeed make waste.)

A product's packaging triggers a certain sensation within us, and most of us don't make a distinction between the package and the product itself. Gladwell provides more examples, like people paying more for round-container-packaged ice cream rather than a square container because they think it tastes better. Another is the little sprig of parsley between the "r" and the "m" on a can of Hormel ham brings the perception of freshness, and peaches in a jar are thought to taste infinitely better than in a can because they look more like the ones Grandma used to make. Gladwell points out that when we put something in our mouth, we decide in the blink of an eye whether or not it tastes good. We are reacting not only to the evidence of our salivary glands but also to the evidence of our eyes, memories, and imagination. This is all done without conscious thought, literally in a blink.

One of Gladwell's observations challenges our concept of free will and what poet William Blake boldly claimed in his poem "Invictus": "I am the master of my fate, the captain of my soul." Gladwell thinks because of the automatic pilot that seems to guide behavior, our spur-of-the-moment actions are largely beyond conscious control, e.g., my lack of control of the next thought that pops into my head and having no idea where it came from. Everyone experiences this. These thoughts of mysterious origin often come without any sense of order. With virtually no space in between them, they can bounce and tumble around helter-skelter like laundry in a dryer, bumping thought against thought. Try to concentrate momentarily on the little chatterbox voice in your head, and you will see what I mean.

The next time you are halfway through a delicious filet mignon and are spontaneously thinking about apple pie and ice cream—while ignoring your guest's world peace comment—see if you can stop the dessert lust long enough to heed the other random thought, visualizing two pounds of sugar going straight to your hips! If the latter can sometimes win the fight, perhaps there is hope for the concept of free will after all!

Our minds are fascinating places to visit. If we are ever to do better at coming to grips with how customers feel about brands, we can heed the words of baseball great Yogi Berra: "You can observe a lot just by watching." I add that we can also hear a lot just by listening.

CHAPTER 4

Mind Plumbing: Becoming Conscious of the Unconscious

● ● ●

SEVERAL YEARS AGO, DANAHER, THE COMPANY THAT makes mechanics' hand tools for Sears, asked our team to help them understand why customers are so loyal to the Craftsman brand. As a good partner, they wanted to help Sears make this legendary brand even more successful. Working closely with the Danaher team, Brandtrust people set out to determine the emotional drivers connected with buying hand tools for both professional and DIY (do-it-yourself) consumers. We probed with our signature Emotional Inquiry (EI) in-depth interviews across three audiences: industrial maintenance professionals, mechanics, and DIY consumers. Among all these groups, EI showed that tools are much more than devices that simply fix things.

EI is an unusual memory-based research technique that effectively draws out the unarticulated emotions associated with experiences, products, and brands. As a skilled researcher guides them through memories and specific moments in time, research participants actually keep their eyes closed and visualize answers. It may be hard to imagine big, burly factory maintenance workers with their eyes closed and recalling their first memories of using hand tools. It might be even harder to imagine many of them teary-eyed as they recall that first experience in their garage or basement with their father or uncle.

The young men's experience with tools is actually a fascinating rite of passage. They often grow up watching a male role model work with tools. They are instantly impressed by their role model's extensive knowledge of tools and amazed at how much these gadgets can accomplish. Tools represent strength, reliability, and power—and men strive to emulate the believed characteristics embodied by their tools. The emotion in the experience causes boys to live for the moment they are asked to help.

To fully put these insights to work, we recommended Craftsman hand-tools be positioned as connections to key emotional drivers: confidence, pride, and honor. The goal was to tie Craftsman to men and their sense of self so they would feel confident and proud of their ability to become self-actualized. These insights are timeless and still relevant today as product road maps in merchandising programs and marketing communications, and the brand continues to hold a commanding share of the market.

Our approach for deeply understanding emotional responses is equally as effective for women. The storied "Jack Daniel's" brand wanted to better understand the unspoken, underlying emotional drivers of female trial, use, and preferences for the brand. The objective of the EI research was to help the Jack Daniel's team better define their female customer so they could get a richer understanding of who she is (and who she is not) and how she feels about what might seem to be a decidedly masculine brand.

What the findings revealed was fascinating: Masculinity is actually not the best way to describe what Jack Daniel's means to people. "Empowering" is a more accurate word to describe what men and women alike truly feel about the brand. It's also a positive, gender-neutral word that represents the connection between Jack Daniel's and a woman's true self—her confidence, independence, and empowered femininity. This insight helped the Jack Daniel's team distill the brand down to three core values: independence, authenticity, and integrity. Men and women aspire equally to these transcendent values that are true to what the Jack Daniel's brand is and has always been. Most importantly, the insights provided a way to attract women to the brand without changing the powerful, iconic essence of Jack Daniel's.

With a much stronger and deeper understanding of their female audience, the Jack Daniel's team created a marketing strategy that aligned with the core values most relevant to women. For the first time in the brand's history, a new product was created and offered alongside the original Jack Daniel's. While the square-bottled "Jack Daniel's Tennessee Honey" clearly illustrates a sweeter taste, the creative label design symbolizes the distinctly familiar Jack Daniel's character. Emotions are stirred with television commercials emphasizing the brand's empowering message and featuring a soundtrack that renews the brand's association with rock-and-roll music. In just over a year, on the market, Jack Daniel's Tennessee Honey became the second best-selling product in the franchise. All of this has reinforced the brand's true essence with loyal customers while attracting new, female, and multicultural customers to the Jack Daniel's franchise. Some things never get old; the best part is, they don't need to. Understanding customers' emotions is one of those things.

Another of my favorite examples is that wonderfully cheesy, perfectly sized, deliciously creamy Kraft Macaroni & Cheese you used to eat as a child. It's perfectly okay to still keep it in your kitchen pantry: Your childhood cravings can carry over into adulthood; you don't even have to keep them a secret. Kraft knows that a lot of their sales for the little blue box come from adults without kids.

In the fall of 2008, Kraft approached Brandtrust with a unique challenge: to understand the latent emotional connection adults share with the perennial kid-favorite macaroni and cheese. Though the product has traditionally been marketed toward children and the mothers who feed them, Kraft needed to understand why a segment of adults were still turning to Kraft Macaroni & Cheese, even though so many other more "mature" options were out there. Brandtrust and Kraft collaborated to uncover what kept these adults coming back for more.

Following the discovery of these insights, we worked with the Kraft team to develop marketing strategies to appeal to adult consumers. We also outlined new ideas for product development and strategies for the entire portfolio. Subsequently, the advertising agency team created a humorous new campaign designed to remind adults "You Know You Love It" and to provide them with a bit of permission to enjoy Kraft Macaroni & Cheese goodness more often.

Throughout our work, on behalf of the world's great brands, we have come to realize something that is absolutely critical: How people say they think and feel is very different from their actual thought and emotional process. They either cannot or will not tell you. Their brains do much of the subconscious thinking and feeling for them automatically. Much more than half the time they might not even know themselves. They feel embarrassed or simply see it as none of your business. As we have seen in the previous chapter, that locked door guards a deep abyss, and often we don't remember where we put the key!

This is the thinking behind one of our most important mantras at Brandtrust, which we keep pinned to the wall of our own minds for constant reference: Shift your mental mode from "voice of customer" to "mind of customer."

Nobody would admit to wearing a platinum Rolex Oyster because it impresses headwaiters and they get a better table. (Big watch signifies big tip.) They are not going to reveal they avoid

Wal-Mart because it makes them feel average or that they go to Saks Fifth Avenue because it makes them feel special even when they can't afford to shop there. I have never heard anybody say they drive an expensive German car because it makes other car owners feel inadequate, or that, apart from Whacko Jack, they wear a particular brand of reading glasses because it makes them feel like Gregory Peck!

A woman is unlikely to tell you the reasons behind her choice of clothing because they help discover and/or symbolize her identity. She will not tell you fashion has transformative social power to help her both stand out from and fit into her social circle. She might not realize these motivations rule her choices. Likewise, a man might not tell you that when he fires up the barbecue, he is heeding an atavistic impulse to play with fire: He is reverting to the proverbial hunter-gatherer, cooking the captured trophies over an open flame. He might even scoff at such an idea as an intrusion into his psychic privacy, yet it is easy for us to see how these could be real but nonconscious motivations we can only uncover with carefully designed motivational research. In fact, these are exactly the motivations our research has revealed.

It is axiomatic that people say one thing and do another. This is not very nice of them, considering you have a job in marketing, but maybe this all-too-common duplicity can be blamed on Mother Nature. When she was figuring out how she wanted us to think, she did not take into consideration that you have a brand to manage right now and a report due next week. This rather thoughtless oversight presents a particularly inconvenient problem for marketing researchers and strategists: If people act on impulse, asking them directly why they choose one widget over another is unlikely to turn up reliable answers. In fact, if we are to get at the motivational mine buried in their heads, we have to dig for it with all the concentrated diligence of a Sigmund Freud. To quote another of Brandtrust's critical mantras: "If you want to know why people do what they do, the worst thing you can do is ask them."

You need to reveal the things people either cannot or do not want to tell you. To repeat mantra #1, just for emphasis, you have to shift your mental mode from "voice of customer" to "mind of customer" to understand what's really going on in there. With the right approach, this can most certainly be done to give you valuable, actionable insight. To truly understand customers, you have to deep-dive into, rather than just snorkel over, emotions.

The old way of herding six or seven complete strangers into a focus group (FG) simply does not reveal what really motivates them. FGs can tell you what people do but not *why*, which is what brand leaders need to know. Dreaded FGs can provide somewhat valid information based on group dynamics, but when was the last time you went shopping with a half-dozen strangers? It's a false premise from start to finish. So, okay, FGs might give you "rationalizations" for what people do, but these rationalizations can lead you down the wrong path. As already stated, we ornery, often-self-deluded humans are well-known to say one thing and do another, particularly when we are in company and even more so when meeting someone for the first time. There's also the problem of that overactive alpha-complex person in the FG who can emerge as the leader to influence the contributions of others. If you get two such people trying to be top dog, you have a real mess on your hands. I've seen it happen time and time again, and it certainly blurs any focus you might be fishing for.

Heaven help you if you get Jack in on it: He hates FGs. He was once invited to participate in a consumer group about pet food. He has never owned a pet in his life, but upon the initial phone call, he said "Yes," he was an animal lover with two cats, a dog, and a canary named Joey and he would love to take part in a focus group. By flirting outrageously with the young, pretty moderator all through the proceedings, Jack threw her off-balance. He also ate most of the donuts set out for the participants, so there was none left for the seven other people, which did not exactly endear him to the group. He excused himself twice to go to the bathroom and made an exaggerated fuss because there were no paper towels. He kept interrupting others to talk about his imaginary canary and how he had taught him to sing "The Star Spangled Banner"—and then horrified the group by telling them he was thinking about farming canaries because they made such a tasty little snack. To cap things off, he loudly and salaciously asked the rather large, elderly, married woman if she would like to get together for drinks when the group concluded. Needless to say, nothing of any use, except maybe advice to screen very carefully, came from this session of the dubious research method.

Jack tells this story with great glee. I only repeat it to emphasize how one FG participant can hog the show and foul up any possible conclusion. When asked why he would do such a thing, he said it was sweet revenge for all the hours he put into the "dumb process." However, he got paid $75 and all the donuts he could eat for the pleasure of wreaking vengeance!

Some marketers might tell you a well-run FG is better than just guessing, but I doubt that; in fact, guessing at least relies on native intuition. Many good marketing people can adopt the art of method acting. They can dig into their own experience to immerse themselves in the persona of the customer(s). They can become the mother looking for the right baby food or the farmer searching out that new tractor and so on, but the really good ones value the kind of focus obtained only from research methods that go deep into the nonconscious feelings of individuals. You literally have to be a bit of a shrink to gain useful, actionable insight; a group grope is not the answer.

An FG moderator can unwittingly prime or mislead a group through subtle and unintended measures. Additionally, without any awareness or guilt of what they are doing, consumers are well equipped for nonconscious deceit. They might want to be approved of by the moderator, seen as perceptive and informative because, without realizing it, they like to be thought of as good subjects. How they feel they are relating to the moderator, either positively or negatively, becomes too important. Of course, the same is true for the questioning moderator who does not want to appear too nosy or personally invasive in managing the process.

While driving to work, you may be strategizing on how to ask for a raise, what you need from the supermarket, or how black holes are actually full of matter. However, if I, as a moderator, ask why you prefer Heinz baked beans over any other brand, you might be totally stumped for a reason beyond liking them and have no reason to think about it any further. After all, who cares why? The question is almost annoying, but it's certain you are unlikely to tell me it's because you had them for lunch one day with your grandpa who loved you when you were three. Unless you're Jack, you most certainly would not hand me the vulgar old quip that every little bean must be heard as well as seen. These kinds of personal answers, however, contain the kind of information I need if I am to advise Heinz on how to keep you full of beans for the rest of your life. I used to joke that market research isn't brain surgery, but I was wrong: It is exactly that.

Again, Brandtrust relies on EI as our own brand of brain surgery, which doesn't involve any scalpels or incisions. Our technique reveals what is happening in the emotional brain and helps our client brands understand what really motivates people and why. The idea is to get at the essential drivers of feelings and decisions related to specific brand behaviors. The methodology is actually derived from psychoanalysis, but we are among the first to use it in a commercial way. We've studied almost every type of physician specialty with EI. Ironically, we've even utilized the technique to understand the deeper motivations of psychiatrists around the world.

Our rational mind wants to believe doctors are scientists who only make medical decisions based on scientific data, but we've discovered that they, too, are susceptible to a gnarly mess of motivations and emotions—just like you and me. They need to feel like confident, capable healers, but challenged by mental disease, out-of-control circumstances, or unresponsive patients, their psychological state can become a tangled emotional mess. Initially, I was concerned the psychiatrists would resist our questions, knowing exactly what we were up to. They recognized what we were doing but actually seemed to appreciate it and, as happily as any physicians we've ever studied, readily submitted to our research probes. Though several psychiatrists ended up in tears, they seem to have enjoyed having their turn to share the deeper reaches of their emotions.

Those being treated are no different. Though our common vernacular terms them "patient," people with health issues are anything but. They are a bundle of negative feelings about their diagnosis, ranging from fear to guilt, anger, and shame to a defenseless loss of control over their lives. Medical mumbo jumbo and unpleasant treatment options leave them feeling bewildered and betrayed by their own bodies. These folks are in such a state that they can scarcely describe their own emotions. Without a research approach, such as EI, we might never figure out how best to communicate with them or help them to navigate their condition.

The EI research method shows many products and services are at parity on the surface. They are virtually indistinguishable to the consumer, but when we dig deep, we can ascertain what is important and what is superficial. We can give real and specific advice on how to communicate a touchstone feature or benefit or the inspiration of a brand ideal. Some examples include helping one of the world's largest retailers to understand why their unique merchandising approach connects with people on a primal human level. EI helped a top auto manufacturer to know what people were really feeling when it comes to safety and environmental issues. A leading air freight company used

EI to identify what small-business customers really expect from a shipping service. One of the world's largest food companies enhances messaging for many of their iconic brands with a deeper understanding of why the brands appeal to people. A large insurance company completely overhauled their customer experience based on insights realized from Brandtrust EI studies. Based on EI findings, a global pharmaceutical company found unexpected ways to encourage patients to actually take their medications as prescribed. There are endless examples of how a deeper understanding of customers can transform a business and drive brand growth.

Over the last 15 years, in thousands of EI interviews conducted all around the world, we have found all people share the most human of values. We've helped a leading credit card company to understand why their successful advertising campaign resonates so well with people and why it will be globally effective. One of the world's largest technology companies asked us to help them understand how they can globally elevate the meaning of their well-known brand. We've explored many brand experiences around the world and discovered that, emotionally, we're far more alike than we are different. We prefer happiness to suffering, warm to cold. We seek love and approval rather than rejection. Mothers and fathers, in all cultures, have similar feelings toward their children. All people of any nationality, race, or religion are, in fact, emotionally similar. There are a finite number of the deepest human emotions, and new ones are not being created.

This universality allows us to apply EI to small consumer samples with the assurance that results will be the same in a larger set. We have discovered that, for the most part, people do not buy products or behave socially because of their demographics. It's simply all about how things and other people make them feel, and we've discovered you can change the way people feel about your brand when you understand what really motivates them.

A powerful example comes from a past project, which was to brand an idea rather than a product. The problem was second-hand tobacco smoke, and as it happened, 98 percent of adults understood the danger of secondhand smoke, but fewer than 4 percent were willing to take any action against it. When the Centers for Disease Control asked us to work with them to turn the situation around, our investigative process and collaborative analysis revealed the way. Conventional wisdom might have been to attack smokers, to portray them as monsters that harm nonsmokers, but the lateral thinking of our process pointed this up as a red-flag direction. Instead, we turned the nation's nonsmokers into a huge lobbying group motivated to attack the smoking environment rather than the smoker. Thanks, in large part, to the integrated marketing campaign, which inspired both the government and nonsmokers to take action, most of America's public places are smoke-free today. If you smoke and hate it when you have to go outside in freezing weather to get your fix, you now know whom to blame.

If you compiled information about how EI has helped companies better understand what makes their customers tick, the number of examples would fill a small book. Our Intel experience is another of my favorites. Walk into any computer store and you're bound to overhear customers talking about the idea of performance. No company knows better than Intel how greatly customers value performance, but what does performance really mean? It's not just about the computer's features or how fast it runs. Volumes of scientific research reveal consumer decisions are often based on emotions and psychological motivations rather than rationality.

In 2009, the marketing team at Intel realized if they wanted to attract customers, as well as gain insights for innovation, they needed to acquire a deeper understanding of the emotional drivers and motivations underlying this critical idea of performance. Intel turned to Brandtrust to provide deep consumer insights that would form the foundation for innovation. Emotional Inquiry actually changed the way Intel thinks about performance.

For this one we went international, with interviews in the United States, Brazil, China, Germany, and India. We helped Intel realize performance is not just about the feeds and speeds of the computer chips: It is the process of taming the chaos in people's lives. It's about preparedness, control, being resistant to failure, and the approval one gets for being all of the above. Performance is about feeling in flow and having everything in harmony. Equipped with an emotionally resonant definition of performance, the brand learned how to connect intimately with consumers. Now Intel truly understands performance is about providing the escape for one to explore various aspects of identity and reaching self-actualization.

The Intel marketing team narrowed the research to four key attributes they wanted their next product to offer: flow, mobility without compromise, design that reflects the user, and security. The Ultrabook was revealed in 2011. The idea of performance was not just applied to the design of the device but also the experience. The product is light-weight, allowing consumers to feel in control. Data flows seamlessly, giving the sense of harmony between the device and the user. There is an absence of chaos, and success is literally at the user's fingertips. Intel's Ultrabook is one of the best examples of deep, emotional insights being translated into action.

It's worth noting that terrible gaffes have been made with faulty, misguided, or in some cases misplaced research. Many people remember Coke's tragic story of New Coke and how people passionately rejected it. In the fall of 2008, Pepsi learned this lesson the hard way when they released new packaging for their flagship product, Tropicana Pure Premium Orange juice. If you drink orange juice (and who doesn't?), you're probably familiar with Tropicana's famous graphic of an orange with a straw protruding from it. It looks fresh and appetizing. This image practically created the category of premium orange juice. It's famous and people love it.

But some lessons are never learned. The decision was made to redesign Tropicana's image to make it more "contemporary" in the infamous words of designer Peter Arnell. You can probably predict the rest of the story. (In fact, a few years prior to this incident, we did predict what happened in work we completed for Tropicana. Apparently, that research did not make its way to the designer's board.)

The designers dropped the familiar orange with beckoning straw and came out with new packaging designs that looked a lot like a generic store brand. The new packaging was, of course, launched with great hope and fanfare until something weird, wonderful, and very expensive happened on the way to the grocery: Tropicana lovers rebelled. They rose up in outrage. They made their voices heard so loudly and clearly that Pepsi had to bring back the old packaging. I love this part of the story because it shows the power of a brand and the possibility for huge passion on the part of its followers.

As advertising columnist Stuart Elliot described in *The New York Times*, "Consumers complained about the makeover in letters, e-mail messages, and telephone calls and clamored for a return of the original look. Some of those commenting described the new packaging as 'ugly' or 'stupid,' and resembling 'a generic bargain brand' or a 'store brand.'" People also complained the new packaging made it hard to find the product in the grocery case. One emailer complained, "Do any of these package-design people actually shop for orange juice? Because I do, and the new cartons stink." Obviously, Tropicana did not need research to determine this could not bode well for the brand. According to Elliot, President of Tropicana North America Neil Campbell stated, "We underestimated the deep emotional bond' customers had with the original packaging ... Those customers are very important to us, so we responded."

But how could a power marketing company like Pepsi, the owner of Tropicana, make a reported $35 million mistake that most likely cost significant market share as well? The answer is simple: They neglected to understand or discounted the emotions customers harbor for their beloved brands. Apparently, for Tropicana drinkers, there is a big difference between an intuitive "grab and go" versus fumbling around the case, trying to find your visual cue: that beautiful orange with a straw that you know and love. The package matters. In fact, most of us do not make a distinction between the package and the taste. We transfer sensations or impressions about the package to the product itself, and the stunningly simple insight is this: In the real world, we often do judge a book by its cover!

Without that big, beautiful orange, you do not have all of the associations you might make with Tropicana—it starts your day, is especially important to your day, has a history and tradition that makes it unique, is indeed 100 percent squeezed—and you are always glad when that first sip goes down. With just a little faith and understanding in this knowledge, think how much time, trouble, embarrassment, and money Pepsi could have saved from the Tropicana packaging fiasco. This story is a great example of how complicated and important it is to find out what people really think. And I say "amen" to that.

The Tropicana team probably tested the packaging and people agreed it looked okay, but no one bothered to tell them it was going to eliminate their sacred orange symbol. There was nothing false or illogical in what Tropicana did, save their testing failed to take into account the way people feel when they lose something they love.

Really good research uncovers lateral as well as linear thinking. This is the more popular way people describe the difference between logical, conscious thought and spontaneous, creative thought. We say people are left-brained if they live a lot in the rational, left-hemisphere side of their brains and right-brained when they rely more on the intuitive, emotional right hemisphere. You live more on the logical side when you write a status report but use the emotional side when writing creatively. It is not particularly scientific. Steve Jobs must have relied on his logical brain to become a computer genius, but he was also a highly creative thinker who, along with a few others of his kind, changed the way the world does its work. The fact is nobody is entirely one or the other: The brain actually works as a highly integrated system, but it does give us a convenient kind of shorthand.

Too much reliance on the rational brain can lead to data and not a thought to think. With the right kind of mind plumbing, the good people at Tropicana might have been able to reveal why folks might not like or buy the new packaging and why they would immediately transfer loyalty to another brand simply because the package had changed.

I do, however, love the image of people rising up with such passion over what in reality (logically) is nothing more than a graphic change: The product was never touched. I somehow imagine them rallying en masse behind the flag with a motto like the famous "Don't tread on me" from the American Revolution. I can hear Tropicana patriots chanting, "Let us to the barricades, boys and girls. Make our voices heard!" There is no more powerful example of how a brand can claim an emotional spot in our lives and how, under ordinary circumstances, we do not spend a lot of time thinking about it until something begins to stink. The Maker's Mark bourbon people faced a similar uprising recently when they thought they could widen the appeal of the brand by lowering the alcohol content. Big mistake. The brand's loyal devotees cried bloody murder and forced Maker's Mark to reverse the decision. The moral here is "Hell hath no fury like a customer scorned and woe betide the perpetrator who does not understand this."

New brands have a great opportunity to get things right from the very beginning, so it is surprising and tragic when they inadvertently get it wrong. In 1996, Home Access Corporation launched its first product after receiving Food and Drug Administration (FDA) approval of an in-home HIV Test. Consumer-products giant Johnson & Johnson simultaneously introduced its version of a similar in-home test called "Confide." Tracey Powell, former Home Access Chief Executive Officer, recounted what happened:

"Both companies had substantial investments at stake—for us over $25 million. Both products were developed at the urging of the Centers for Disease Control and fast-tracked for FDA approval because extensive quantitative research indicated pent-up consumer demand and public health concerns. Our company, and I'm sure J&J, which is a stellar marketer, had undertaken significant consumer research to determine purchase intent, pricing sensitivity and several other market factors. However, we failed to do any emotional research even though our advertising agency had advised we should. When the agency tested our ad concepts, they suggested we give away free test kits as a 'thank you' to the consumers who participated. They quickly discovered we had a very serious problem when every consumer refused the free kit. We literally could not give them away. This was in the days before we had drugs to manage HIV as a chronic disease and, because of the social stigma, a positive diagnosis was psychologically worse than a death sentence. And our product was the messenger. Had we done the emotional research, we would have known about the problem before our launch date and maybe before it was too late."

Both products were launched and failed to show positive momentum in the first six months. Within a year, J&J had exited the market. Smaller and more flexible, Home Access was able to adapt quickly and turn their test into a business-to-business product now sold to state health boards, prisons, and various public health agencies. Needless to say, the failings of conventional market research created an unpleasant and costly experience, estimated at losses of well over $100 million, for these companies.

As a brand advisor, I feel for the guys who had to make the decision to, in one case, fold their project and, in the other, to drastically reduce expectations. The money involved was considerable. It only shows that doing the right kind of mind plumbing, before the project got too far into development, would have avoided both red faces and the wrath of shareholders. There was nothing wrong with the premise, but, unfortunately, there was much falter with the choice of consumer research. Maybe the rational brain held too much sway over the emotional. What sounds logical in theory often makes no sense in the wild and crazy world of feelings.

Emotional motivation is fascinating because we can rarely explain it. It's not logical in the usual sense of the word. It can be difficult to ascribe to any kind of origin and is often totally spontaneous, e.g., the boy who comes across an accident where the roof of a truck is stuck under a bridge. While a group of adults stand around, scratching their heads, trying to figure out what to do, the boy solves the problem by thinking laterally: He simply lets the air out of the tires so they are low enough to get the truck unstuck. My friend and sometimes editor Monique Ethier gave me a lovely word in French to describe this kind of person: *débrouillard,* somebody who can think outside the box with uncommon common sense.

Even without the benefit of research, lovely flashes of insight sometimes come to us with no rhyme or reason, and they can be worth a fortune. Some bright Vlasic Pickles soul solved the pesky problem of how the standard sliced pickle can make you say a bad word when it falls out of a sandwich into your lap. That's why only 3 percent of the billion sandwiches made annually in American homes contained sliced pickles, which would hardly seem fair if you were Mr. Vlasic. The fabulously simple solution was the kind that makes you want to commit suicide because you didn't think of it: slice the pickles vertically rather than horizontally. This "duh" idea became a hit: "Sandwich Stackers" had sales that reached $60 million in the first year alone. After 15 years, I bet that number increased exponentially.

We sometimes come across what I call "brand serendipities" that are equally delightful and fortuitous. In *The Tipping Point: How Little Things Can Make a Big Difference*, Malcolm Gladwell writes how the Hush Puppies shoe brand was saved from extinction by events its managers had no hand (or should I say foot) in creating.

In late 1994, the Wolverine people, who make Hush Puppies, were thinking of booting out the brand that made them famous because sales were down to 30,000 pairs a year and going nowhere. For some weird reason, however, sales suddenly started to pick up in New York City. It was discovered the brand was suddenly "hot" in bars and clubs in downtown neighborhoods, like Soho and Greenwich Village. A couple of the brand people discovered the ball got rolling because a handful of hipster kids in the East Village were buying the shoes precisely because no one else would! These anonymous young men started a fad that turned into haute couture. In 1995, the company sold 430,000 pairs; in 1996, it sold four times that amount; the next year, it sold even more. There was no advertising to persuade people they should start wearing the Hush Puppies because they were cool. It just happened in a very big way. Jack tells me he even saw Hush Puppies stores in several fashionable malls in Buenos Aires this winter, and he asks, "Who woulda thunk it?"

Gladwell continues:

> "The shoes passed a certain point in popularity, and they tipped... *The Tipping Point* is the biography of an idea, and the idea is very simple. It is the best way to understand fashion trends, the ebb and flow of crime waves, or, for that matter, the transformation of unknown books into best sellers, or the rise of teenage smoking, or the phenomena of word of mouth, or any number of the mysterious changes that mark everyday life is to think of them as epidemics. Ideas and products and messages and behaviors spread just like viruses do."

Sharp introduced and sold 80,000 low-cost fax machines in 1984. More and more people bought them until there were so many, it made sense for everybody to have one. The fax tipping-point epidemic came in 1989, when Sharp sold two million machines in the United States alone, and I don't know how many other brands were on the bandwagon by then. They seem to be following the buggy whip into obsolescence, but I read recently that buggies are apparently still used in Japan, where a rapidly aging population resists change.

Think about cell phones: They got smaller and cheaper all through the 1990s; service got better and better as sales began to increase. Suddenly, there was a tipping point and everyone had a cell phone. Now that they are minicomputers, cameras, and navigation devices, as well as phones, we cannot bear the thought of separation. Nobody seems to be able to go 10 minutes with his or her smart phone out of reach. In our super-connected lives, we take them everywhere—many people even sheepishly admit to sleeping with their phones.

I read about a woman who had her cell going so she could tweet during child labor. She apparently did not want coworkers to think she was a slacker just because she was having a baby. "Crackberry" was the prophetic name we gave to Blackberry addiction. The iPhone came along, and now an entire generation spends more than half its day with a bent neck, looking down at an object in their hand. Just think what it will do to human evolution. It took a gazillion years to learn walking upright, and it could be all for naught. On the upside, however, our thumbs could become much more dexterous, with all that texting, Googling, file-checking, gaming, and punching in phone numbers. We should make a pact, though, that if we can stand the pain of separation, we might want to pocket our devices and keep them turned off the next time we go to a dinner party on a Saturday night!

A tipping point is when a brand dream is made in heaven, and it is not as random as you might think. Brands all have to start somewhere, and that somewhere is usually with a single person. Gladwell describes such people as "mavens and connectors."

Mavens are people who gather price and product knowledge and feel compelled to store the information in their heads. Jack, who has no idea of the cost of even the most common supermarket purchases, has a maven friend who can repeat from memory the price of a can of beef broth as it is sold in three different supermarkets. How he does this nobody knows. His memory for such things is phenomenal. And he gets great pleasure out of sharing this information. The same person is a font of product knowledge. If you need to know the difference between Samsung, iPhone, and Blackberry, he is the one to call because he knows all the details, including where to get the best price.

Mavens are an important factor in spreading brand information, and preferences are often the start of something big. Mavens have insatiable curiosity. They study supermarket fliers. If there is a discussion on anything from the weather in Argentina to who was the victor in the Peloponnesian wars, Jack's maven is always at the ready with his cell phone to Google the answer and feels compelled to do so, right on the spot.

Connectors are like mavens, but they have a huge digital Rolodex of friends and acquaintances and enjoy linking their network to products and prices. They are more actively involved in getting people together over ideas and products and have a knack for being listened to. A connector, for example, will go to a restaurant, return home, access his address book, and then email everybody who lives near the restaurant to let them know how good it is. He might even let them know, while he's still *in* the restaurant, by sending them photos attached to his Facebook message. If he switched from Apple to Samsung, he would email everybody he knows with a cell phone about the difference.

When you look at the phenomenon of Hush Puppies' reincarnation and how it started with a few kids in lower Manhattan, you get the idea. You probably know a person who has what we call style. It's a trait much bigger than just fashion. A person can be fashionable but not stylish. Style requires a personal stamp for authenticity. A few stylish people may indeed be the impetus behind the entire fashion industry. They may even influence the star fashion designers who seasonally lead us by the nose, and a brand can take an active part in getting such a ball rolling.

What if the Hush Puppies brand manager had gone into the streets to visit a few bars and clubs, simply to observe the popular, stylish, and charismatic person followed by other people? Could one be found and persuaded to wear the shoes as a brand ambassador? For a bit of money and free product, all that person has to do is wear the shoes and only comment on them if asked, which in the case of Hush Puppies most certainly would have happened. This is like using word of mouth from the mouth of an informed and influential person, literally direct marketing.

Brands in many categories do indeed send ambassadors from their own ranks into bars and pubs to promote beers and other spirits. It's always a good experience when a beer rep comes into a pub, buys a round, and has a bit of a chat with the customers. Such people are specially chosen because of their social skills. Avon and Tupperware built big brands with highly personal and festive direct marketing. Ford has just hired 100 socially connected young people armed with new Ford Fiestas to spread good words about the product. Talk about the consumer now being in charge of the brand!

These examples bolster the argument that brands are social instruments and the salient artifacts of identity. The more we understand the true motivation for their adoption, the more we can refine a course of action to get them into people's lives. The depth of the ocean is an exotic goldmine of life we cannot even imagine; so are the depths of your mind.

•

CHAPTER 5

The Principles of Principals: Doing Well By Doing Good

●　●　●

THOUGH I TOUCHED ON THIS IN CHAPTER 2, THIS topic is worth a great deal more than those few words for the simple reason that an effective brand's most important reason for being comes in the articulation of its purpose or mission. A mission is no longer an exclusively internal consideration to be shared among the brand's personnel. It is not something you write casually and pin on the boardroom wall for occasional reference. If it is to be pinned anywhere, it is on the minds of everybody—from your employees to your customers and all other stakeholders forevermore. It is bigger and more critical than a brand's practical performance promise as usually expressed in advertising. In a nutshell, your mission must be the driver of your brand's performance and the touchstone of its present and future success. If we want our brands to play a part in people's lives, we do this most effectively through the practice and public expression of how it ideally contributes to their lives.

A "mission" is the expression of what your brand stands for; in fact, a better word would be "ideal." People respond to others who live according to like principles and ideals. There is plenty of evidence to suggest they do the same with brands. In fact, you might even think of your brand's ideal in terms of a higher calling, and it works only when you feel it in your bones and live it in the here and now.

Business associates I talk to about this accuse me of "gilding the lily." They say companies just make products to sell stuff, and it need go no further in our thinking. One correspondent went so far as to say this: "I am not a fan of 'higher calling.' It is altogether too presumptuous, arrogant, and close to messianic. These are, after all, just companies, products, and services, not a new religion or life creed. I also think that they set themselves up for moral failure rather than delivering themselves from it."

This point of view is not necessarily cynicism but simply incredulity that commerce can serve any kind of higher purpose. When I get this reaction, I think of Sophocles' observation from a couple of thousand years ago: "The unexamined life is not worth living." The cause of death might well be birth, but between these two monumental events, a great deal happens in our lives to suggest we do indeed live by more than bread alone.

When I ask my well-meaning critics if they take pride in their work, aim to give good value for their wages, feel that what they do makes a valuable contribution to the companies they either run or work for, I always get a knowing look that seems to say, "Okay, but not everybody feels that way, and people do cheat." My response is if they do not feel that way, they will soon be out of a job or out of business and so will any brand that does not observe the common decencies of doing the same. These are virtues that require a great deal more than lip service on the part of an individual. We expect nothing less of the brands we choose to bring into our lives.

The point is brands have to mean what they say and what they say has to be realistically within the purview of their capabilities. Phoniness does not work. It never has and never will, but is it possible that IBM people mean it when they say, "Let's make a smarter planet"? I think they do. I think it is what we might call their higher calling.

I agree that brands have to be as they say they are and must measure their words carefully. An astute young man I know said, "One thing corporations try to do is get us to 'please like us' on Facebook, but this is a big mistake. Facebook is a useful tool, but there is an unwritten etiquette to it all, which corporations attempt at their risk because if it's not authentic, we'll know. This is partly why young people are starting to feel that Facebook is not cool."

Since this insight comes from a tech-savvy guy in the most receptive age group, I think it is worth listening to and looking out for with all due diligence. I suspect, however, he is thinking about obsequiousness and pandering, which does not work person-to-person or (as Facebook would say) friend-to-friend online. When it does, we can hardly blame the technology any more than we can blame the telephone company for obscene phone calls! The message is many companies have to stop pushing the digital conversation the way they are used to doing with paid media.

In *Wikibrands: Reinventing Your Company in a Customer-Driven Marketplace*, Sean Moffitt and Mike Dover state, "Some business leaders argue persuasively that customers do not want to engage with brands, believing that consumers are tired, cynical, and overwhelmed by them. In some cases, this viewpoint is not misguided. After all, not many people desire a deep relationship with their dishwasher soap. However ...

marketers who follow 'brand burnout' theory will do so at their peril." The authors go on about how passion for brand engagement is not evenly distributed but is instead concentrated in small pockets of activist consumers whose influence can sway public opinion. These consumers are not necessarily a niche or fringe. They are the 1-to-10 percenters who blaze trails and make it their business to market to others, as we saw in Gladwell's *Tipping Point*.

As Moffitt and Dover point out, marketers have not been good at incubating brand engagement, so it is not surprising that many consumers doubt the sincerity of their reaching out. The brand being vitally and truly interested, so customers are not the *objects* of brand communication but are more like *extensions* with valuable insights and enthusiasm to share. And to get the customer to engage with the brand requires different skill sets for listening to and talking with customers as equal partners.

My personal feeling is that natural people, who do not adopt a corporate pose, are more likely to see themselves not as companies or even brands but as the equivalent of neighbors doing what Jack would call "having a bit of a chat" with other neighbors. Why should we feel that brand leaders, who are on one side of the counter, are different from customers, who are on the other side? This relationship is the strength of a brand. For example, the British food company Innocent has customers that "enjoy" engaging with Innocent, and vice-versa. This relationship comes naturally because the brand is just that way. Natural (as in genuine and unaffected) is its DNA. It's sort of like the Tom Hanks of branding!

We see a strange kind of division in a lot of business correspondence written as though it's addressed to aliens. Jack has the best advice when he says to write a business strategy as though you were talking to your mother. He once said to me, "If I told my mother that we should 'leverage our relationship for maximum mutual advantage,' which could be biz gobbledygook for 'love each other a lot,' she would have hit me on the head with her cast-iron frying pan." Are some people afraid of clarity because it might appear to be too simple, or do they wear verbal obfuscation as a mask to hide what they really feel?

Brand collaboration is also more accepted by the Millennial Generation accustomed to social networking on Twitter and Facebook. As the influence of its members grows and widens, so will digital activism across all age groups, e.g., taking your young daughter out to buy new winter boots, and she undoubtedly insists on her desired brand of choice and will "die" if she doesn't get the exact one. You can bet your boots all her friends will get a text message turning them green with envy because when you indulge her dearest wishes, it will be the brand they all covet. Sharing this kind of news over the digital backyard fence is now second nature to your daughter because she can tell many people (friends) all at once. Staying connected is "sort of like, I mean, you know" a matter of life and death.

One ordinary household brand that gives women reason to feel in touch is Dove soap with its "Campaign for Real Beauty." The people at Dove's ad agency (Ogilvy & Mather) discovered that only 1 to 3 percent of women around the world had the self-confidence to describe themselves as beautiful. This shocking revelation was true, even in countries we normally associate with having beautiful women. Janet Krestin, Ogilvy's chief creative officer, used global research to help the brand create a public debate about whether beauty is skin deep. It was "the first time anybody had taken the pressure off of women and told them, 'Look after what you have because what you have is great.' We didn't want to replace one beauty dictatorship with another, so there was no finger wagging or preachiness. We threw it out there as a question and let the audience participate. As a beauty brand with a history of being real, simple, and visual, we felt there was a powerful idea/question we could legitimately pose."

The execution of this scenario included a powerful video called *Evolution*, which shows a model's flawless beauty being "manufactured" in stop-motion and with digital enhancement. It got more than 10 million hits on YouTube. Other Dove films showed young women talking candidly about body image and unreal expectations. In 2006, Dove took the campaign into new territory with the Dove Self-Esteem Fund, aimed at helping girls and women to feel comfortable with their own beauty and even further by questioning the Western concept of beauty altogether. If Dove does not exemplify the power of doing well by doing right and thriving in the process of doing it, I do not know what does. It's a brand story that is hard not to love.

Someone else who loves the power of mission for both individuals and companies is Michael Saylor, CEO of MicroStrategy. He has said that small missions produce small companies, but great institutions survive because their missions are timeless, ethical, and imperative. Of his own organization he once said, in *Fast Company* magazine, "Our mission is to make intelligence accessible anywhere." In the same article, he talked about what he says to new recruits: "Call some friends tonight, and ask what their company's mission is. Then ask yourself, would I follow that organization to the end of the earth? Or is it simply a place to spend 40 hours a week?"

Most businesses write what they think is a working vision of what business they are in, where they want to go, and how they want a product to be perceived, but unless this is articulated and activated in terms of a life-improving ideal, they are falling short of a brand's potential. Insight into this process comes from how well you understand the people most important to the brand's future—both customers and employees—and how you can attract them to a brand that contributes to their lives in a truly meaningful way. There are three questions to ask about your mission statement: What is its value to your customers? How does it affect the way your employees feel about their company? How does it promote *esprit de corps* and a willingness to innovate in the ever-challenging face of change?

The Body Holiday in Saint Lucia is a resort that combines the best of a luxury beach vacation with a comprehensive wellness center that has won awards as the number-one destination spa not just in the Caribbean but also in the entire world. If founder Craig Barnard were to communicate these facts alone, the resort would probably be successful, but he sees a much larger role for the brand's ideal. The resort's chosen mission is to provide guests with the lasting skills they need to maintain a healthy balance between body and mind that will stay with them long after their tans have faded. Indeed they have the opportunity to acquire skills they can forever call upon when events of their busy lives back home leave them feeling up to their knees in alligators of stress that can put their natural balance out of whack. This powerful brand ideal is brought to life with one line: "Give us your body for week, and we'll give you back your mind."

This ideal resonates with potential guests and serves as a potent reminder for previous guests. It is a promise the staff of the resort can get behind: Every one of them is trained to live it. It allows The Body Holiday to command a premium price, only because it lives up to the promise made. Occupancy during winter months is consistently 100 percent, and it remains high even during summer months when other resorts are half empty. An unprecedented number of guests come back for a repeat performance time and time again for years on end. One of the things I find most interesting is that the promise was written 25 years ago, but when it appears in the resort's advertising, it still makes the phone ring off the hook.

Such is the appeal of a powerfully articulated mission that promises and delivers a contribution to people's lives. "And improvements never stop," says marketing director Andrew Barnard. "Most people say, 'If it ain't broke, don't fix it.' We fix it anyway. Both our physical surroundings and the content of the experience receive constant improvement and substantial investment."

I find it fascinating that this small business instinctively stumbled upon a principle that supports Stengel's position: "If you are not ambitious enough to want to make a big difference in people's lives, you won't make a big, positive difference in your business. Ideals move millions, along with politics, war and peace, art, technology, science, and maybe mountains." The thought here is "go big or go home."

"Give us your body for a week, and we will give you back your mind" is not the campaign for this year: It is the driving force behind the brand's very existence. Like all great ideals, it is unlikely to wear out or get old having already lasted a generation. The brand people may never have to change it, because the message touches on timeless motivations. It will stay that way as long as The Body Holiday's people breathe it daily and it is a big enough concept to keep them fully engaged. An ideal is often something staring you in the face, but like the workings of our minds, it remains opaque until some gifted soul comes long to uncover it. I refer to it as a "hidden truth."

Sophisticated brands like The Body Holiday and IBM aren't the only ones able to follow such a script: Everyday products like Dove soap can also discover and embrace meaning in people's lives that sets them above and beyond the ordinary. I can't think of a brand less lofty than a disposable diaper. Its obvious purpose doesn't inspire poetry, but under the leadership of Jim Stengel at P&G, it went from a product invented to keep babies dry to one that plays an important part in keeping a child happy and comfortable during a crucial phase of development. This is the touchstone that mothers can be drawn to, and it has made Pampers the dominant brand in its category. Once more, the purpose of a brand ideal inspires a high level of customer engagement.

Stengel tells the story of a UK brand, Innocent, that was started in 1999 by three friends who met at Cambridge University. They went into jobs in advertising for a while before they decided what the world needed was a food company that "made it easy for people to do themselves good." Their way of doing this was to make fruit tubes; juices; vegetable pots; and convenient, delicious, healthful fruit smoothies. As young guys, they were not eating particularly well and decided casual food was a great way to get the world going in a better nutritional direction.

I love this brand story because it's a bit zany. (I cannot help but feel I would like to meet the founders for coffee.) Their 30-year goal is to become "the earth's favorite food company." Innocent might just do so because of its unpretentious approach to business and life in general. The company reminds me of kids huddling together to run a lemonade stand. They talk to their customers the way they talk among themselves. They had a banana phone when they first started the business, and they still use it. Anybody in the company can answer it to talk to a customer. They invite people to "pop over for a visit" and people do. They have what they call "annual grown-up meetings." Everybody in the company sits "all mixed up." There are no departments. They also invite 100 customers to come in on a Saturday to invent new recipes. The idea is for everybody to be authentic with no posing. Anybody in the company can speak for the brand, and they go to great lengths to find people who are comfortable doing just that. The brand is expanding into Europe with the same principles, and the business is growing rapidly, so much so that in 2010, Coca Cola bought 58 percent of the company.

The willingness to do good is good for the soul and the value of the brand. Stengel reports that in 1980 brand value did not contribute much to the market cap of the S&P. It is now the biggest asset category in both business-to-consumer and business-to-business. As Stengel suggests, if you are not managing and measuring your brand against a brand ideal, you are consigning it to the middle of the pack. Embrace the idea with heart and soul; dominate your category. His 10-year growth study of the 50 top brands shows operating on the principle of making a difference in people's lives improves business growth by a whopping factor of three.

In 2003, P&G lost $85 million in market cap in only six months. Google's charts show that it went down to about $146 billion. That's when CEO A.G. Lafley asked Stengel to take on the job of global marketing officer, and he devised five examples of brand ideals that influence growth:

1. Eliciting joy
2. Enabling connection
3. Inspiring exploration (new visions)

4. Evoking pride

5. Impacting society (challenging the status quo)

By helping P&G people to apply this kind of thinking to figure out how life influences business and business influences life for all their brands, the parent is currently worth $250 billion. As the cow said to the farmer, "That ain't hay."

Stengel gives us dozens of examples of brands that pursue an ideal for the benefit of all. Some are quite touching. All show what you need to do is emphasize brand health, where you stand with customers, as much as you do financials. Again, how you make people feel is the number-one priority. Even as far back as 1939, William Hewlett and David Packard saw the value of working from values. They determined their business had to make a contribution to society, which kick-started all of Silicon Valley. As Stengel says, keeping that flame alive is what has made Hewlett-Packard go from a worth of $5 billion in 2001 to $35.4 billion in 2011.

Finally, I would be remiss if I didn't state the brand ideal of the company I founded and remain with as CEO. I started my career in advertising agencies and had my name on the door of Arian, Lowe & Travis, a Chicago-based firm that achieved considerable acclaim for creativity. Being a creative exec made it easier for me to make the transition from a focus on "messaging" to "meaning." Advertising, by its very nature, is concerned with how the ads make people feel, so I felt the need to devote my time and energy to helping companies get a deeper understanding of what makes their brands tick in the minds of their customers, beyond the limitations of focus groups and 30-second TV commercials.

Brandtrust Beliefs

We believe people want to make a difference in the work they do. Businesses can serve noble purposes and become powerful forces for positive change. We believe deeper human insights inspire businesses to create solutions, promote positive change, and provide opportunities for people to live better lives in a better world.

Our unique promise to our clients is, in working with us, you will change the way you think about your customers and how you can make a difference with your business. Our simple brand ideal is that by revealing deeper human truths, we help businesses become positive forces.

An effective way for your business and brand to think about a higher calling is, strangely enough, to frame it as if your company were a nonprofit organization. Under that circumstance it is not concocted as meat for an ad campaign. It is not a marketing gimmick or public relations stunt. Instead, it very likely emerges from the brand leader's beliefs and convictions long before the brand is successful. In fact, the mission is likely what motivated the brand's start in the first place.

As a result, when a higher calling guides a business to success, it makes a lot of nice noise. People admire you. The press calls for a story. The best workers come looking for you instead of the other way around. Analysts rate and respect your integrity. Investment gurus trust and recommend you. There is a buzz on the street, spreading far and wide. People like me write about you with a certain type of awe. Publishers ask you to write about yourself. You get invited to be on CNBC with Larry Kudlow. Without intending it, you strike fear into the hearts of your less-focused competitors. Your good fortune gives you no place to hide, and the limelight puts an added glow on your brand's mystique.

"Mission" reminds me of the story about the guy who looks up to heaven and asks, "God, how come the world is in such terrible shape? All this hunger and poverty and wars and disasters. It's awful. Why don't you send somebody down to fix it?" Suddenly, the guy hears a whisper in his ear and realizes it's God's whisper: "Ah, my friend. I did send someone: I sent you."

Everybody who deals with your brand—employees, customers, suppliers, the press et al.—is waiting to be your willing missionaries, given the stimulus of a potent mission.

Give them one.

CHAPTER 6

Social Media and the One-to-One Revolution

• • •

SINCE I PUBLISHED MY FIRST BOOK ON BRANDING 13 years ago, I find it strange to realize digital technology was then in diapers. It was clear the book still had good bones but badly needed a transfusion of new thinking. I thought it could be done with a bit of rewriting and judicious editing, which, with my writing partner Harrison Yates, I proceeded to do.

Fat chance.

After a couple of months of struggling, I found the process to be like taking a 1999 car with 500,000 miles on it and trying to make it a sleek, new 2013 model. More accurately, it was like trying to make myself run and jump like a 22-year-old against all odds of possibility. We bid farewell to most of the old book. "Out with the old and in with the new" is the 21st-century situation faced by a lot of established companies.

The fact is it's a whole new marketing world out there, and with the rate of change being what it is, I could be feeling the need to redo this book five years or less from now. As Moffitt and Dover state in *Wikibrands*, "In today's business climate, cultural adoption of change has never been more agile."

In the same book, Moffitt and Dover plot the evolutionary progression of branding from the first registered trademark in 1860 as a mark of ownership, e.g., cattle, to something you can buy, then to something desired for ownership to something trusted to something preferred to something you want to something loved to now, when it signifies something you participate in. This progression mirrors the journey of the brand from one controlled by its maker to one now controlled by its users. It is this latest incarnation of marketing that was largely missing from the pages of my old book.

It's not that preferences, trust, and desire have gone away; instead, attributes claimed by the brand are no longer blindly accepted. Feelings are still at the heart of branding success. More and more, customers define the brand with the feelings and attributes they most admire and/or require. A woman might covet a pair of Prada shoes and the Jaguar automobile that seems to go just right with them, but her brand approval is significantly more her own affair than the makers'. She might indeed feel entitled to correspond directly with the car's chief designer about her chosen model, with full expectation that the designer will respond. If she contacts the president of Prada to make sure none of the brand is made with Third World child labor, she better get a satisfactory answer. Add to this that a click on her computer keyboard enables her to check out other owners' satisfaction with Jaguar rather than her going on the faith of the brand's word. She is a partner in her chosen brands; she knows it and wants the brands to know it, too.

The simple old days of brand management by a brand's managers have gone bye-bye. These brand's managers no longer work for the brand: The brand's users do, and those users feel free to express what they want the brand to do. For the uninitiated, this is a difficult concept that doesn't seem to make much sense until we read about the Maker's Mark bourbon kerfuffle, where users kicked up a storm about the brand people watering down the formula to give it what would be, in the brand people's eyes, broader appeal. The same thing happened when Tropicana messed with the packaging and disregarded their customers' feelings. These are not accidental incidents. They signify the customer's insistence on participation and brand ownership. People are saying, "How dare you mess with what is mine! How dare you think you can just go and do what you want to my brand without my consent!"

Brand people have changed along with this shift in control. We see fewer and fewer Complaints Departments because everybody in the company can be the Complaint Department. As we saw in the delightful example of Innocent, everybody can answer the banana phone to talk with a customer. Just as customers want to participate in the brand's business, the brand people want to participate in the customer's lives—like Starbucks, Zappos, Amazon, and other brands that go out of their way to create interactive communications. The brand and its users are collaborators. They work together in partnership to define and improve the experience. This is reflected in Cisco CEO John Chambers' remark: "... [P]roductivity growth is going to be about collaboration and network-enabled technologies. Our customers are candidly driving this. They've said we need to understand better what you are going to do, where you are going to interoperate, where you are going to compete."

The next revolution in branding may be brands becoming members of the family! Or maybe our customers will actually be on our payrolls!

The message of the brand is now bigger than convincing you of a benefit that makes your product better than anybody else's. It is now also concerned with questions of integrity, authenticity, candor, transparency, and the reliability of the brand's word. The ability of the consumer to evaluate these qualities has never been more possible or more acute. Creating relationships has taken over image creation. The watchwords are "participation" and "engagement." Do you remember the "Four Ps" of the old marketing: product, place, price, and promotion? They have gone to marketing heaven, where they, I hope, rest in peace.

Brands now ask customers to have a hand in product innovation. Frito-Lay has customers inventing new flavors for Doritos. If your invented flavor won the contest, you could have walked away with $25,000 and 1 percent of sales in perpetuity. Brands also invite customers to create TV commercials to air during the Super Bowl. Innocent invites their British customers to invent new recipes. If you're not asking your customers in, you may find your brand stuck in the old paradigms, wondering how it happened and wondering even more how your brand can ever compete again.

The world's languages have changed along with the old conventions. To use a simple example, we click on an application, download it, and store it in the Cloud. Listen to techies talk as they do in what they think is normal conversation—it's like a foreign tongue nobody would have understood even 10 years ago. For somebody fearful to venture into the new branding paradigm, doing so can be understandably intimidating. We now use Google, Twitter, YouTube, Bebo, Orkut, Facebook, and LinkedIn—and eBay's 90 million members take part in online auctions for more than $51 billion worth of merchandise every quarter. Once we get used to it, we take it all for granted.

Even company names have gone a bit berserk. Who in their right mind would call an online shoe company Zappos? What on earth is a Vevo? A Twellow? A Hulu? A Vimeo? A Pinterest? A WhatsApp? A Kik (which apparently has 40,000 users and counting)? Your 10-year-old daughter probably knows even if you don't. It's all a very far cry, to say nothing of refreshing, from General Motors, General Electric, General Mills, and all the other old five-star generals who salute you with names from the 19th Century. And what is a Wiki brand? Moffitt and Dover give us the definition:

"A progressive set of organizations, products, services, ideas, and causes that tap into the powers of customer participation, social influence, and collaboration to drive business value. Derived from the Hawaiian word *wiki*, traditionally meaning 'quick' but more currently meaning 'tribal knowledge' and 'a collaborative website,' and the Middle English word *torch*, whose current business meaning is 'a distinctive name identifying a product or manufacturer.'"

The way *Wikibrands* implements this definition to engage customers with participation is nothing short of astonishing. Chicago publisher Sourcebook Press has an application that lets you alter a children's book so you can include your child's name throughout. Other publishers are following suit. Libraries are making e-books available for lending. Anybody can create a video on any subject, including a brand experience, and you stand a chance of its going viral on YouTube with millions of hits. Moffitt and Dover write about the creators of the *Potter Puppet Pals*, who post skits based on the denizens of "Hogwarts." Their most popular video has been viewed more than 80 million times. As Moffitt and Dover say, "Eighty million people, by the way, would be enough to qualify as the fifteenth most populous country in the world." It goes with YouTube's meritocracy where anybody can get their 15 minutes with the click of a few computer keys.

A remarkable story of brand participation through mixed media is attributed to Canada's M&M's candy. The *National Post*'s Holly Shaw reported it as an example of a great idea. It is all of that, but I repeat it here as a 21st Century textbook case of how to put multiple sources of media to work for collaborative social involvement and the kind of fun that any candy brand might envy.

It started as an idea when Renee Rouleau, the former creative director of BDDO Proximity Canada, became enamored with Google Maps. He saw Google Street View as an "amazing, immersive, unique, awesome experience." It got him thinking about how to use it in advertising and in particular how to get M&M's into some of the shots that would be on Google Maps for years. The Google camera car does not announce its arrival, so, aiming for a bit of crazy luck, he took to the streets on a hot summer day, dressed in a giant M&M suit. When that didn't work, the agency put a big red cardboard M&M's "spokescandy" in front of the windows of 30 employees' houses around Toronto.

Bingo! The Google camera picked up three of them. This led to a virtual scavenger hunt contest called "Find Red" that, as Hollie Shaw says, "tested the boundaries of both the legal and digital development departments."

The "Find Red" campaign idea was to sleuth out where Red was hidden. The prize was a red Smart car. The agency made a video that explained how it all worked on YouTube, Twitter, Foursquare and Facebook, along with downtown posters and bar codes on M&M's packages that could be scanned for Red's location on the Google Street View app.

The campaign was a big hit with social media users spending more than four times the industry average—more than 19 minutes—on the "Find Red" website. It also racked up 8.4 million media impressions and 225,000 Twitter mentions and was a marketing first that won a ton of awards, including a top Cannes Lions advertising prize. Needless to say, people enjoyed it no end. It's also worth noting "Find Red" was the brand's first foray into a major social media initiative, which proves two things: The growing importance of social media as a branding fundamental, and an old-brand standby can indeed learn new tricks. I congratulate parent Mars on this success.

As with a great many effective ideas, other brands soon saw the wisdom of using social media. Volkswagen launched a contest asking drivers to find as many VWs as they could on the roads of South Africa. A Mercedes-Benz "Escape the Map" contest asked drivers to find a fictional character, Marie, inside Google Street View's map of London.

A big part of the old paradigm was the focused brand. To avoid any kind of confusion, the brand name had to be focused laser-like on one product category. Apple's focus was computers; Amazon's was books; Zappos' could be nothing but shoes. This has changed to an emphasis on tribal connection and shared group values as in "I am an Apple fanatic. What are you?" Focus has changed from a product lineup to a values lineup. Being the genuine article in character is just as important as the product's facts. This allowed Amazon to become the world's biggest department store, selling anything and everything online, including the kitchen sink, as long as they do it on time and with fantastic service. No one knows the bounds of Apple's imagination or what game changer they may offer next. Whatever it is, the Apple tribe of consumer partners will be chomping at the bit to get at it.

Nike CEO Mark Parker makes it clear when he says, "The ability to connect with consumers is the most important competitive advantage in business today." It certainly did not hurt Barack Obama in the last presidential tussle with Mitt Romney. The Obama team was well-versed in the ways of social media while the Romney guys were apparently left at the starting gate, staring at the rump of the digital Democratic donkey going at full gallop down the track. It would be wrong to say a mastery of social media won the election for the Obama team, but when you think what it did to get the uprisings of the Arab Spring off the ground, its power as a political tool is undeniable. The Romney people were like old media going up against the rambunctious energy of the Internet. In that scenario, old vs. new is hardly a fair fight.

There is also the Old Spice story and how the new media can work with the old when some outstanding TV commercials were adapted to run alongside social media to generate more than 10,000 YouTube channel views; more than 150 million downloads from other places on the Web; 800,000 Facebook advocates; and 100,000 Twitter followers—all in a matter of weeks!

Tell this kind of thing to Jack, who refuses to be impressed and asks, "What's a YouTube?" He knows, of course, but he enjoys being contrary and going against the stream. He also said he always thought he was the last man on earth to use Old Spice, and he's not sure he likes all those other people cashing in on the secret of why women find him so attractive.

Like Groucho Marx, Jack would never join a club that would have him as a member, which is why he stubbornly rejects joining Facebook or LinkedIn. He remains suspicious of technology's grip on our lives. He agrees with Op-Ed columnist Maureen Dowd, who wrote in *The New York Times*, "Everybody is connected to everybody else on Twitter, on Facebook, on Instagram, on Reddit, e-mailing, texting faster and faster, with the flood of information jeopardizing meaning. Everybody is constantly connected to everybody else in a hypnotic, hyper-din: the cocktail party from hell."

Despite Jack's and Maureen's views, the concept of brand tribalism is a fascinating one. We do think of ourselves as Chevy guys, Bud guys, Armani gals, and Jack Daniel's guys, and can you name a more inclusive tribe than the devotees of Harley-Davidson, which has to be the cult brand of all time? It is strange to think the company nearly went under 35 years ago.

AMF could hardly give the brand away when it was sold to 13 Harley execs in 1981. It is now a $5 billion company and can't make enough of the iconic machines that are "a little special, a little mysterious, a little bad." Owning a "hog" literally represents a lifestyle and a source of identity. A Harley is something you wear; the Harley logo is indeed the most popular tattoo in the United States. We used to brand cattle as a sign of ownership; now we brand ourselves as a sign of belonging.

Even before the inclusive nature of today's social branding phenomenon, there were 800 chapters of the Harley Owners' Group (HOG) with a quarter-million members. They hold regular meetings and put out a bimonthly newsletter. They attend club meetings, as well as go on outings sponsored by dealerships. There is a "Ladies of Harley" subgroup for the 10 percent of Harley owners who are women. Rallies, including a spring Bike Week in Daytona Beach and a summer gathering in Sturgis, South Dakota, draw tens of thousands. Company personnel and dealers are part of the rally and club action, which gains them close contact and important opportunities for two-way communication with customers. The brand never takes their customers for granted and regards them as the company's most valuable asset. If there was ever a need for evidence that brands are all about feelings, Harley has to be it.

This is the way of all great brands. Real, dynamic, heartfelt customer engagement is not a frill or marketing add-on: It is the passion of every great organization. It is the essence of branding and social media that makes it more possible than ever to get it right. Companies face significant brand erosion if they do not pursue a concerted effort to take part in the one-on-one conversations available through social media. As Moffitt and Dover point out, only 8 percent of people trust what companies say about themselves, and only 17 percent believe companies take their customers seriously. Ironically, people who actively engage in social media were twice as likely to believe companies were interested in them. These are shocking numbers, but at least there is a suggestion that social media is the way to go for better customer contact and the inculcation of trust.

Retail, of course, is still a powerful medium, and some online retailers are beginning to see the value in adding storefronts to their marketing mix. This is particularly true in categories like eyeglasses and shoes (sorry, Zappos), where customers feel it is safer to try before they buy. Online retailer ClearlyContacts, the world's largest online source of contact lenses and eyeglasses, has a high-service model allowing customers to return purchases with no charge for shipping. Opening physical stores becomes a catalogue brought to life. EBay did something similar in London. Best Buy seems to be moving away from big-box into smaller, scaled-down venues as a showcase for online purchases. To better meet the needs of city dwellers, giants Wal-Mart, Whole Foods, and Target are developing urban stores with smaller footprints and trimmed-down assortments. Piperlime, Gap's online-only retail subsidiary, opened a store in New York's chic Soho district that allows customers to try before they buy through the Internet. The number of new marketing options never ceases to amaze me.

But, of course, it's not old media vs. new media. You now need to use all the media available to take advantage of the many touch points customers can encounter on the way to a purchase. A person watching a TV commercial for the Toyota Camry might immediately use her mobile device to Google "sedans," which might in turn pop up a paid search link for Camry and other car reviews. She then clicks through the "Car & Driver" website to find reviews, which might turn up a YouTube video that somebody made about their Camry and maybe the "Camry Reinvented" Super Bowl commercial that played earlier in the year. The next day, while driving to work, she sees a Toyota billboard. When she gets home, there might be a direct mail piece in her mailbox offering a limited-time deal. She then calls a friend who has a Camry to get his opinion before she goes to a dealer for a test-drive and finally buys the car.

MarketShare CEO Wes Nichols describes this process in his March 2013 *Harvard Business Review* article, "Advertising Analytics 2.0," which examines how different ads interact in their contribution to sales. A company he worked with used MarketShare's new, highly sophisticated analytics techniques to discover that "TV ate up 85% of the budget in one new product campaign, whereas YouTube ads—a 6% slice of the budget— were nearly twice as effective at prompting online searches that led to purchases. Search ads, at 4% of the company's total advertising budget, generated 25% of sales. Armed with these rich findings and the latest predictive analytics, the company reallocated its advertising dollars, realizing a 9% lift in sales without spending a penny more in advertising."

Several things are revealed in this quote: There are now many more ways to go than with just the old standby of conventional media; you have to know how all the parts work collectively to drive sales; the parts can and should be juggled to deliver the best results. Nichols describes the old way of measuring each media part separately as "living in swim lanes." When a marketer knows how advertising touch points interact dynamically in real time, sales improvement can go 10 to 20 percent higher.

The one-to-one revolution has brought exciting times. The tools it brings to the branding party give both brands and customers enormous newfound power to enter into absorbing give-and-take communication for the benefit of all. People still discount what many brands have to say, but brands now have new tools to sharpen their focus so that ring-true ways to improve the dialogue can be discovered. Make no mistake: Persuasion is still the business of marketing, but we are glad we can go about it in more human terms. Jack's definition of advertising—"having a bit of a chat with the customers"—proves to be prophetic for all our marketing endeavors.

CHAPTER 7

The Art and Practice of Persuasion

● ● ●

EVEN WITH THE PLETHORA OF MEDIA CHOICES available and the finest analytics to measure media effectiveness, brands are still stuck with how to make themselves welcome in people's lives. In order to do that, we have to think more about how people actually live their lives. As media consultant Jeffrey F. Rayport says in an article in the same issue of the *Harvard Business Review*, referred to in the last chapter, "To win consumers' attention and trust, marketers must think less about what advertising 'says' to its audience and more about what it 'does' for them."

"Shortly after the U.S. presidential elections," explains Rayport, "Fidelity placed full-page ads in major newspapers that posed the question 'How could the election results affect the markets?' and invited readers to download insights from the company's expert panel." Another Rayport example comes from

London-based beverage giant Diageo, when they devised labels for its Brazilian-market whisky that turned the bottles into a conduit for custom video:

> "Timed to hit the shelves for Father's Day, the labels enabled a gift giver to scan a code and upload a video message for Dad to the cloud. Dad could scan the code with his own phone to receive the recorded good wishes. The video promoted the brand, tightened social bonds, and allowed the company to reconnect with both giver and recipient for future promotions—events, tastings, offers, and the like. Diageo transformed the most basic form of advertising—a label and a logo—into an open-ended personal message system that could be woven into consumers lives."

These are examples of what Rayport calls in the title of his article "Advertising's New Medium: Human Experience." They demonstrate how a brand can indeed be welcomed into our lives in ways that differ from pushing and shoving what we used to call the "Unique Selling Proposition" at customers with repetition upon repetition as the method for achieving success.

Persuasion is as important as ever, but it is now necessary to fit it into the way people live their lives rather than how the brand lives its life. The new media can have dramatic effect on how it is done. For example, the Diageo Father's Day promotion would never have been possible even a few short years ago, and it is likely that the sheer availability of the technology was the impetus for the creative solution. The same goes for M&M's Google Map "Find Red" promotion, which we know was initiated by the very existence of the technology.

As Rayport says, "In a media-saturated world, persuasion through interruption and repetition is increasingly ineffective. To engage customers, advertisers must focus on where and when they will be receptive." He separates timing opportunities into four spheres: the "public sphere", where we move from one place or activity to another, both online and off; the "social sphere," where we interact and relate with one another; the "tribal sphere," where we affiliate with groups to define our identity; and the "psychological sphere," where we connect language with specific thoughts and feelings.

When Zappos put ads in the bins used to move your belongings (including shoes) through airport security checks, its advertising is in the public sphere; same for Charmin when it put temporary public restrooms in Times Square during the holiday season; and again when Duracell rushed its people into areas devastated by Hurricane Sandy to provide mobile charging stations, supply Web access, and give away batteries. These activities do not sound like advertising, but they probably do as much or more to persuade than even the best TV spot, simply because they occupy an appropriate moment to make real contribution in people's lives; they undoubtedly get a lot of play in social media from appreciative customers. I do not know what the Zappos bin ads said, but I hope it was something like, "Don't you hate it when you have to take off your Zappos?"

A good example of communication in the social sphere is the Diageo "talking bottle" that I'm sure warmed the heart of many a dad on Father's Day. There was also the Old Spice video ads shared by millions online to delight friends, solidify connections, and create interaction.

Harley-Davidson is as good an example as any of the tribal sphere, where the brand promulgates identity, self-expression, membership, and empowerment. From Hermes, Gucci, and Louis Vuitton, luxury brands accomplish the same ends when their devotees badge themselves with logo-festooned products as displays of status. Toting a Lord & Taylor shopping bag around

Manhattan sends a different message than a bag with a Wal-Mart logo. And no symbol speaks more than Rolls Royce's flying lady perched on its distinctive radiator, announcing to the world you belong to an exclusive, limited-membership club called The Very Rich.

The psychological sphere is where all advertising operates in one way or another. As Rayport says, "Ads in this sphere provide new ways to articulate ideas, engender habit formation, guide reasoning, and elicit emotion." E.G. Nike's "Just do it," Apple's "Think Different," Budweiser's "Whassup," IBM's "Think" and, many years ago, Volkswagen's "Think Small" along with Alka-Seltzer's "I can't believe I ate the whole thing." Could you name the brand if I asked you, "Where's the beef?" These concepts encourage habit and establish a cognitive beachhead that connects a brand to a mood or emotion. They are like the pop song you can never get out of your head. They are what we call "sticky." Every copywriter wishes he could write just one very sticky line in his lifetime.

As Rayport explains, the four spheres sound similar to what you might find in conventional ad campaigns, but they take a customer-centric approach rather than a media-centric route. Instead of focusing on which media to emphasize in a campaign—television, Web, mobile, outdoor displays, etc.—marketers should start by determining how advertising can integrate into consumers' lives in ways that deliver value and win their trust.

Time, place, and mood are more important than ever, but equally so is the marketer's attitude. Advertising must approach consumers with deep respect for their ability to discriminate. Customers are not tools invented for the convenience of brands: They are you, me, our families, and our friends. Nobody ever lost a dime by overestimating how smart we are. I have known marketers who think we are an amorphous herd willing to be brought to heel. Just feed us the right message, point us in the right direction, and we are easily recruited on board the brand. Some have even expressed disdain for the common intelligence, which is no way to think about the source of your daily bread and butter. I am willing to bet a large sum, no matter what you think of the most ordinary person's cranial capacity, you have never met anybody who thinks of themselves as stupid. In fact, the stupid one is the one who thinks others are stupid! If you do not appreciate your customers, if you neglect to understand how your brand makes them feel, you will never win them to your side.

It's been said that social media has turned every business into a mom-and-pop store. I love this thought: It's a good way for even the biggest brands to think about the customers they may never get to know as personal friends and neighbors they can invite to the house for beer and popcorn to watch the Super Bowl. This brings up the point that we still get together to watch conventional TV for news and favored programs.

Just think of how you feel about your favorite show, and it's easy to understand the continued attraction. Retailers Neiman Marcus and Target even teamed up recently to co-advertise on a popular ABC show; the cast was even hired to perform in commercials. This is an unusual and expensive way to go, but integrating the advertising into the show made the ads impossible to miss.

Standout drama is also the best advertising for the networks themselves. Think what the *Downton Abbey* series does to sustain PBS with donations from viewers. Perhaps being under threat will spur the networks to start putting on quality programming that may keep them alive. After all, we once thought television would put the movies out of business, but it hasn't. New ways of viewing are surely waiting in the wings to change everything. A company called lvl (an abbreviation of *level*) is working on ways to make interactive television. If you watch hockey, the company has a system where you can use lvl's live second-screen application on your iPad to vote for who you think will score in a shootout. When you watch the Oscars, you will soon be able to use lvl TV platforms to access real-time information and interact with other fans on social media. lvl president Jean-Francois Gagnon says, "We're making television more exciting, more relevant." He sees a great future for TV as what he calls a "display medium." As one technology begets another, who knows what innovations wait in the wings to keep our eyeballs glued to the screen?

The National Post's Diane Francis tells us the story of "How old media gave away the store":

> "The biggest heist in history was when newspapers and magazines allowed Google Inc. to 'crawl' their content to readers, to pay nothing and to sell ads around their stories ... But Google and others are not finished. They now stalk television and cable and are beginning to make major moves to disintermediate both and provide video content directly to viewers. The business model under attack is monopoly cable companies that make

roughly $2,000 a year from the average subscriber. But this hegemony ended in 2009 when the technological Rubicon was breached and television signals became digital, not analog."

She goes on to say that within the next decade or so, the Cable Guy and the Newspaper Delivery Guy will disappear, but information and entertainment will be cheaper and more plentiful for all.

Netflix CEO Reed Hastings says in a *National Post* interview, "TV in the future will be like a giant iPad. It will have a bunch of apps on it, each app will have a unique experience... [W]e're getting beyond the just a stream of video, which is all broadcast technology can do, to really try to be more innovative about the interaction ... [Y]ou're going to open your iPad and there is going to be a bunch of different networks." When asked if he worried about the inevitable arrival of competition, Hastings said this:

> "You have to accept in business that you're going to have a lot of competition. There aren't any interesting markets where you're the only car company or the only newspaper. So, you know we got out in front early because we saw

the opportunity about Internet television ... but we never thought we're going to be the only one. Because there is too much other content. We don't have sports content, news content, music. And there is lots of other types of content that people are going to want, and that is not what our brand is all about."

New options may at last free up the wasted time of flipping through a hundred channels to find something you actually want to watch, often without success. We know Netflix now has 33 million subscribers paying only $7.99 a month for a veritable cornucopia of on-demand entertainment options. They can choose to skip commercials altogether, but we have yet to discover how much technology will affect advertising's creative process. We do, however, get glimmers of it here and there when we see how *Millennial Males'* social media comments about eating Cinnamon Toast Crunch at night formed the bones of a minicampaign. The main target consumer for the cereal is mothers buying it as breakfast for their children, but the social media division of ad agency McCann Ericson (cleverly called "Always On") saw the chance to create highly relevant posts on Facebook and Twitter to get a lot of engagement from males with cheeky comments like "Good in bed" and "Spoon with me." Twitter seems to be replacing Facebook as the preferred social media platform. As columnist Jonathan Kay has said, "Facebook is still useful for people like me: middle-aged types looking to catch up with college friends' baby pictures, but many current college students have let their Facebook accounts lapse into disuse, and some high school students aren't even bothering to sign up. The site has become too popular with their parents' generation to be cool."

People who have never been around the ad business are curious about its creative processes. After all, they see dramas about the advertising business, often multiple times, on their home screens every night but never even imagine any of the people who create them, which probably has a lot to do with the success of the wildly popular *Mad Men* TV series—a show that gets Jack fired up over its inaccuracies. He says, "We boozed a lot in those days but rarely in the office, and we didn't treat women like sexual chattels. We were never as slick and greasy as the guys in that show and, I don't mind saying, not everybody had a mistress."

If you ask him to explain the process, however, he will tell you greater media choice has not changed it all that much: "Technology has, in many ways, reset the creative button, but after all is said and done, somebody has to come up with the big idea and how to best execute it in any of the chosen media—and in my not-too-humble opinion much of what passes for advertising should be executed as violently as possible!" Jack has won dozens of awards for creativity in advertising, so, at least in this case, he does not speak from ignorance. He says it starts with a detailed brief he uses to ask and answer four questions:

1. Who are we talking to? (Audience)
2. Where are we now in their minds? (Current Perception)
3. Where would we like to be in their minds? (Objective)
4. How do we get there? (Strategy)

Questions 2 and 3 are best framed in the voice of an ideally defined customer. They are most effectively arrived at through research, like Emotional Inquiry, that gets into the customers' heads in truly meaningful ways. When EI is not available—clients often skip this critical step either for lack of funds or believing they can simply do without it—Jack relies on life experience and his natural ability, as a total ham, to play the role of the person on the receiving end of the delivered message:

"It's all about the audience, which is why I start with the assumption they want nothing to do with my stupid ad. You have to be able to put yourself on the receiving end of the message to measure if it rings true or grabs you or confuses you or bores you stiff. You have to have an involvement meter in your brain. The worst sin is irrelevance, particularly the boring variety. Once the brief is done, a copywriter sits with an art director and they talk about what they did last night and where they should go for lunch and how there is no quarterback they would rather be than Tom Brady (well, you get the picture) until one or the other breaks the ice and says, 'What if we said *this*?'

And then the other says, 'Hey, I like that but how about if we said *this* and showed a shot of so-and-so?'

It goes back and forth like this until they get a 'eureka moment' that feels right. It can happen quickly or sometimes over lunch, or sometimes one calls the other at 2 a.m. and says, 'What about *this*?'

The other replies, 'What about you not calling me in the middle of the night?'

Other times they sweat for a week or more until they can say in their bones, 'That's it!' Once they feel they have the right answer in the form of a headline and illustration idea, each one goes to his respective craft to flesh a concept out with the appropriate words and pictures."

Since I was once an ad agency owner and have worked with Jack, I can say his description of the process is vastly simplified but more or less accurate. He does, however, leave out the most important part of that process: When he talks about finding the "eureka moment," what he really means is the moment of maximum surprise. Effective communication always involves you with an unexpected hidden truth. It has to have crystal clarity, but always with the ability to engage you, to make you do a double take, to carry you to a moment of revelation. I emphasize these words to impress upon you their importance for how brand managers might look upon the work their ad agency presents to them. If it does not consistently follow this prescription, you need a new agency. If it does, ask them to marry you.

Jack probably leaves it out because all the really good ad creators take this part of the process as a given or second nature. It is what we mean when we use the business cliché "the ability to think outside the box."

We enjoy hearing and telling jokes because of what makes them funny. What makes us laugh is the fact of a surprise, a twist at the joke's punchline, e.g., "A horse walks into a bar and the bartender asks, 'Why the long face?'" Jack loves telling this joke because, in very few words, it paints a vivid picture with a surprise verbal ending. Likewise, the judicious use of humor in advertising gets attention and makes a brand feel accessible and likable. In the past, humor was thought of, by serious marketers, as frippery. Old-time ad guru John Caples once said, "You can entertain a million people and not sell one of them. There is not a single humorous line in two of the most famous books in the world, namely the Bible and the Sears Roebuck catalog."

Well, Mr. Caples, the Old Testament is admittedly not a bellyful of laughs, and the Sears catalog is not up there with rib-ticklers like Tina Fey's *Bossypants*, but so what? Humor is simply one way we communicate, not an end in itself. Certainly there are as many lame varieties of it in advertising as there are up on a stage full of comic improvisers.

Humor can be a bit like music. Famous ad man David Ogilvy disliked jingles because, in his opinion, they don't "sell," which leads me to believe he never saw the commercial in which a platoon of young people congregate on a mountain side, holding candles while singing, "I'd like to buy the world a Coke." How would he explain the mnemonic musical attraction of Alka-Seltzer's "Plop, plop, fizz, fizz, oh what a relief it is" or the ubiquitous "bong, bong…bong" that signals Intel inside?

Humor comes in many forms and guises. Jack was once assigned to write a commercial for a waterproof workboot. He and his art director first went the usual route, thinking of boot-clad feet splashing through puddles and mashing through mud, with the song "Singin' in the Rain" in the background, to make the point. While this was a perfectly acceptable concept and might have done the job, they were not happy because it was predictable, expected, or not convincing enough. They kept going back and forth until they arrived at the very simple, close-up visual of a hand tossing a muddy boot onto a polished table then slowly pouring a jug full of water into it. The trickle of the water was the only sound, except for the announcer at the end who said, "Sorel Boots. If the water can't get out, the water can't get in."

This makes an involving and therefore effective 15-second TV commercial, but like most good ideas, it also lends itself to print advertising, a subway poster, in-store display, adaptation for YouTube, etc. A simple but compelling and memorable demonstration of a hidden truth, it proves the point with a wry story and makes people feel they can trust the boots to keep their toes dry.

A more current example of lateral thinking in communication comes with Jack's assignment to rebrand an idyllic beach resort in Saint Lucia. Working very closely with the resort management, he saw an opportunity to create a vacation experience geared to the modern career couple who live life up to their knees in alligators of busyness. They juggle their time between big jobs, spouse time, the clamor for attention from the care and feeding of children, the running of a household, and the modern necessity of ever-present, never-off-the-grid digital connectedness. The pressure of the ticking clock and end-of-day exhaustion make opportunity for marital intimacy a scarce commodity. For such people, luxury is no longer measured by what they can own but by time itself. In order to remain sane, they must learn to steal the luxury of time. With this sympathetic attitude in mind, Jack and his client decided to call the resort "Stolen Time." The headline that would dominate their communication would be "The Holiday of Stolen Time."

Jack got designer / art director Gerald George in on the act: They came up with the idea of illustrating the proposition with Adam and Eve in paradise as portrayed in classical art but with the twist of their talking on cell phones. To communicate the idea of toxic busyness, they had Eve asking, "Wanna do a meeting?"

Adam responded, "I'll have my people call your people." This is a very different approach from the usual resort advertising showing a beach and happy people gamboling in the surf, which is what most resorts do with the result that they all look the same.

I don't know if you can actually teach people to think outside the box, but you can encourage it by nurturing a playful attitude within your organization. Even if your employees work in accounting and prefer numbers to words, ask them to get together and come up with ways to advertise your product. Make it a collaborative no-holds-barred game in a setting where the participants don't have to worry about being laughed at or censured if they come up with a lousy jingle; encourage them to go crazy. The purpose is to ignite the creative side of their brain. Who knows?! You just might get a great idea! Try giving the group a problem to solve. For example, a new competitor has just arrived on the scene with innovations that make all our products obsolete. What do we do? Make it so there are no wrong answers. When I question Jack about this, he thinks it's a great idea; it's exactly what he does when he is working with an art director to come up with a great ad.

Metaphor plays a big role in our everyday speech, as well as in brand thinking. Stolen Time is such a metaphor aided and abetted by the visual of Adam and Eve talking on cell phones to illustrate busyness in a way that successful adults can understand and empathize with. What may appear on the surface to be funny is in fact a quite serious proposition. Jack says, "I used to define advertising as a salesman who comes knocking on your mind instead of on your door. This is not a bad metaphor, but in the light of what we have learned about how customers see their favored brands, I would now say advertising and branding in general is like romance: It is the search for a passionate, lasting engagement that ends up in wedlock."

I love what Bedford Cheese does with its cheese descriptions. This small retailer has two stores: one in Brooklyn and the other in Manhattan. Next to every cheese, in the display case, is a metaphoric description of its provenance. They say of Mastorazio—a new sheep's milk cheese that comes from Italy—"This Lindsay Lohan of the cheese world, this pecorino, has a tan leathery exterior that surrounds a delicate yellow paste with hints of herbs and the aroma of hay. You can almost hear the bleating of Lindsay up in the Italian hills." Another is for a cheese from a California dairy: "Icelandic ponies, Japanese cats on the Internet. Yawning puppies. Toddlers who give each other hugs. Goats climbing all over everything. Pink and green macaroons. Red pandas. Sparkling nail polish. Do you get where I'm going? Cute things. This cheese is so perfect and cute and delicious it makes you feel like you want to marry it."

To me, this is retail branding of a very high order. It expresses a love of cheese with the same intensity of a sommelier writing about vintage wines. It states, "We know and love our cheese and hope you will trust our recommendations." It shows in spades what can be done with the simple medium of a glass display case to attract trial. It is romantic and lovely to the eyes and ears—people feel affection for the brand. I cannot help but love these Bedford Cheese stores for how they speak to me with such metaphoric richness and originality.

Metaphors are more than figures of speech. In his book *I Is an Other: The Secret Life of Metaphor and How It Shapes the Way We See the World,* James Geary tells us we use metaphors every 10 to 25 words. They are how we make sense of things we want to communicate to others. In fact, recent linguistic theories suggest all language is essentially metaphorical. They become as natural as eggs cooked sunny-side up, raindrops that feel like butterfly kisses, falling off a log, or any other metaphor you care to insert here. We can't shake them because mental modes or schemata are the basic components of implicit memory. Metaphors are a kind of shorthand that helps us to rapidly connect and convey mental modes. Words are patterns in the world, as are melodies, cars and houses. With language, we take learned patterns in our lifetime and transmit them to children and tribe.

Brand names are metaphors in that they quickly convey what a product or service means so we can instantly attach a mood or feeling to them without much thought. We are linguistic pattern-making machines, and, in many ways, brands are products manufactured not in factories but in our own imaginations.

Vivid metaphors are essential to good communication. I heard somebody recently say, "I couldn't sleep last night; my head was full of bumblebees," which is a lot more interesting than the usual "I had a restless night." Metaphors make speech highly memorable because they convey a visual experience. You can actually see and hear those bumblebees treating your skull like a hive, but we have to be careful about overuse, mixing them up and stringing them together in dreadful, overused, clichéd language. In modern biz speak, our language takes on bizarre shapes, as in "At the end of the day, moving forward, there is light at the end of the tunnel where we can pick the low-hanging fruit to leverage a doable meeting to get a viable outcome." If I could remove overused metaphors with the flash of a wand from today's business vocabulary, the list would include the following words and phrases: leverage, moving forward, light at the end of the tunnel, at this point in time, low-hanging fruit, price point (what's wrong with just plain price?), and out-of-the-box, which I have several times used with extreme guilt in this book. I might even delete the suddenly ubiquitous word *awesome* from the dictionary until its faddish appeal disappears. Vivid sunsets can be awesome. The annual migration of Monarch butterflies is awesome. The talent of Michelangelo is awesome. The contemplation of everlasting life is awesome. However, the installation of a new granite kitchen countertop; a new dress; or a dark, rich, new craft beer can be extremely pleasing but hardly the inspiration for awe.

Words count. How you use them says a great deal about whether you are a follower, a leader, a conformist or an original, a thinker or merely a trendsetter—and we can safely say the same for the words of brands. Take a leaf from my book on that one. The rule rings true—crystal clear and iron clad. It's as obvious as the man in the moon.

CHAPTER 8

Visionary Leaders

● ● ●

IN THE PAST, A GREAT MANY BRANDS JUST HAPPENED.
To the delight of their inventors, some brands claimed a unique
spot in the marketplace without the noise of mass media.
Around the time when just about the fastest thing moving was
a horse, brands grew with no more than the march of time
and the determination of an imaginative leader. Think Coca-
Cola, Levi's, Ivory Soap, and General Electric. Through effort,
imagination, innovation, and some marketing skill, awareness
spread over the metaphoric backyard fence and these names
became brands by the grace of time's patina.

Today, of course, brands still start as they did back then
with a specific purpose devised by an imaginative leader. But
success depends more and more on going beyond something
developed for mere consumption, and the speed with which
their inventions find a place in our lives is vastly quicker. Jack

Dorsey started a brand called Twitter. Remarkably, in a mere five years, Twitter gained 200 million users. Now he has introduced Square, a device that allows you to use a credit card on your cell phone or iPad. Just watch this one go ballistic.

Products are now more likely to be brought to life by a hand-in-hand leader's values and convictions in the form of a unique vision. Names like Amazon's Jeff Bezos, Apple's Steve Jobs, and Starbuck's Howard Schultz spring to mind as leaders with extraordinary vision.

Starbucks CEO Howard Shultz has more in mind for his company than designating it as a coffee and pastry shop. In his own words, "What Starbucks created around coffee is an extension of the front porch. If you look at the UK, the English pub is an extension of people's homes but for a different beverage."

It is hard not to see that this vision plays a huge role in Starbucks' success way beyond a place to get a good cup of java. Schultz made getting coffee an experience, an event, a social happening. He gave it a mystique you *felt* when ordering your favorite brew and watching the barista do his stuff with exotic, hissing coffee machines. Before Starbucks, nobody in North America had ever used the word *barista*. Coffee was something you took either black or with milk—and it often tasted like gasoline. To the person behind the counter of a regular coffee shop, asking for "Peppermint White-Chocolate Mocha" or a "Cinnamon Dolce Frappuccino" would have drawn blank stares. Now these are just two of the beverages you can experience from a brand that has become the world's largest coffee purveyor with nearly 21,000 stores in over 60 countries and a valuation of $17.1 billion you can largely attribute to the vision of one man.

Not long ago, we never knew anything about the people who ran our favorite brands. Now they develop the kind of status and awareness that was once the exclusive reserve of movie stars and politicians. News of them is almost as important as what they sell. (Steve Jobs was a good example.) They are the source of news as futurists. We do not find it at all unusual that they are becoming some of our most important philosophers. With some obvious and notable exceptions, they are moralists and even humanists in their attempts to understand the inner workings of our lives. It's not just business people who devour the words of Jack Welch, Jeff Bezos, Warren Buffet, and scores of others.

MIT's Peter Senge once described it as "our ideas of leadership, and in particular, the cult of the CEO-as-hero." He went on to say it is a cult that forms a "pattern that makes it easier for us to maintain change-averse institutions. When we enact the pattern of the CEO-as-hero, we infantilize the organization: That kind of behavior keeps everyone else in the company at a stage of development in which they can't accept their own possibilities of making change. Moreover, it keeps executives from doing things that would genuinely contribute to significant change. The cult of hero-leader only creates a need for more hero-leaders." Senge says further that the hero-leader is the one with "the answers":

> "Most of the other people in the organization can't make deep changes because they are operating out of compliance rather than out of commitment. Commitment comes about only when people determine that you are asking them to do something they really care about... [T]he new leaders are less likely to see themselves as 'the person at the top'. That definition says that leadership is synonymous with a position. And if leadership is synonymous with a position, then it doesn't matter what the leader does. All that matters is where the leader sits."

Senge goes on to define leadership as simply "the ability to produce change."

Then, of course, there is the innovative-narcissist business leader driven to seek power and glory. Psychoanalyst Michael Maccoby once described them in the *Harvard Business Review*. They are usually independent and innovative. They are often charismatic orators who attract followers and, although they seek adulation, they are not easily impressed. They are welcomed when the going gets tough; however, they tend to be a bit paranoid. Rather than teach, they prefer to indoctrinate. They listen only for the kind of information they seek. Their faults grow as they become more successful. They are not good at bolstering your self-esteem. If you work for one of them, it is best to work to his vision. He likes praise but easily spots a sycophant. Disagree with him only when you can demonstrate how he will benefit from a different point of view. Either do that, or quit for the protection of your own mental state. Silicon Valley seems to breed these kinds of genius-driven leaders. Think CEO superstars like Bill Gates, Andy Grove, Steve Jobs, or Larry Ellison. Recall how an executive at Oracle once described Larry Ellison: "The difference between God and Larry is that God does not believe he is Larry."

There will always be bosses who are hard to work with or for, but fortunately for the workers of the world, the leadership ethic shows signs of change. Asking rather than telling and collaboration rather than autocracy bring a new meaning to how we spend a huge chunk of our days. Some more-progressive companies can even be called employee-driven, which is a refreshing change from the antics of a royal boss (and maybe a royal pain) like the Sun King Louis XIV, who said, "My greatest concern is for my own glory."

The accumulation of huge wealth has also been democratized with the advent of riches spawned by dotcom startups and the rapid growth of new companies that is possible today, but creating personal wealth is likely to be a by-product of creating wealth for customers. As reported in the *Financial Post*, in his book *Liar's Poker*, Michael Lewis said what defines the rich today is not the conspicuous consumption that was the mark of earlier generations but conspicuous production. The Golden Age's top 1/10 of 1 percent made a show of wealth, imitating the landed aristocracy's extravagant indolence. They commissioned gargantuan neoclassical monuments to themselves and adopted the trappings of royalty. In contrast, the new generation of rich, mostly young males, make a life of work.

A dramatic example of exponential dotcom growth is illustrated by the remarkable fortunes of Instagram founder Kevin Systrom and his partner Mike Krieger. As reported in *Vanity Fair*, with the help of some startup funds, in just 18 months, they and their 13 employees built a company with 30 million customers who downloaded the app on their iPhones. The story gets truly dramatic when, in 2012, the partners sold the company to Facebook for $1 billion: $300 million in cash and the rest in Facebook stock! As *Vanity Fair* editor Graydon Carter writes, "The poignant coda to the story, and one that says so much about the disruptions brought about by the Internet, is that Kodak, the company that invented the portable camera and, indeed, invented the digital camera, in 1975, filed for bankruptcy last year just two and a half months before Instagram was sold to Facebook."

While there is good cause to celebrate the triumph of Instagram, there is also something sad when an iconic brand like Kodak disappears from the common consciousness. It's a little like losing part of the landscape or a vital part of our experience. After all, George Eastman's Kodak put the family snapshot into the albums of ordinary people in the same way Henry Ford put the family automobile on the road for our very recent ancestors.

Indeed, moments of our most personal histories captured in photographs were called "Kodak moments," an expression that has virtually disappeared from our vocabularies. While the company continues to operate quite successfully in the field of corporate digital imaging, the sadness of its fall from public visibility exemplifies the sentimental attachment we have to the artifacts of our histories and the powerful feelings that brands engender.

Another big acquisition came along in the spring of 2013, when Yahoo! bought the blogging service called Tumblr for $2.1 billion and its founder, 26-year-old David Carp, put $250 million into the pocket of his hoodie. Carp, who had never graduated from high school but was addicted to computer tech from a very early age, apparently does not care at all about the money, except for what it can do to develop his company. He continues to live in what has been described as a "cramped Brooklyn apartment." Seemingly, even with their healthy dose of good fortune, the young Systrom, Krieger, and Carp will not be retiring anytime soon.

As American author and game designer Neal Stephenson once said in *Inc. Magazine*, the new high-tech leaders enjoy wealth, but they have interests other than wealth:

"Clearly, most have motives other than having a big house on the edge of a country club, motives that are incredibly diverse. Some have long-term social goals, some dream about something they want to build, and starting a company is how you get things done now. These are people who tend to be very active intellectually and whose personal goals go way beyond the desire to be the president of a company. Being the founder and CEO of a company is something they do in order to achieve their real goals."

Is there a lesson here for all of us? Does it tell us that making pots of money is not an end but merely an outcome and that keeping our eyes on the mission rather than the remuneration is the real way to improve the compensation? Steve Jobs lived somewhat modestly: Though he had more money than King Tut, he resided in a nice but fairly humble house on a pleasant but not ostentatious street in Palo Alto, California.

The guys we are talking about here mostly go around in jeans and a T-shirt. You have to wonder if they own a tie or even a pair of socks. They appear to drive their own cars without the aid of a chauffeur. Instead of driving a Maserati or Bentley, they likely drive BMWs or Porsches, preferring big, shiny brains to big, shiny rides. I love when a leader like Amazon's Jeff Bezos compares the rise of doing business on the Internet to the Cambrian Era in evolution because, as he said, "That was when the earth had the greatest rate of new life. What people don't know is that it also had the greatest rate of extinction." This suggests to me he is a lot more than a high-tech guy with a vault full of money, that maybe he has read a few of the books he sells – one who thinks not about what he has done but what he still has to do. Bill Gates does not sit around counting his pieces of eight. He and Warren Buffet teamed up to give away billions, and they work hard at doing the right thing and making a difference in the world. Beyond professional brilliance, there's a lot to admire about these people, something we can all think about on the road to our own vision of success.

Fast Company once ran an article called "Make Yourself a Leader," which listed the following 12 steps:

1. Leaders are both confident and modest (you have an ego, but you make the people around you more powerful).

2. Leaders are authentic (you know who you are; you believe in yourself; you walk the talk).

3. Leaders are listeners (you are curious and know that the enemy of curiosity is grandiosity).

4. Leaders are good at giving encouragement, and they are never satisfied (you raise the stakes for everybody; you're always testing and building both courage and stamina throughout your organization).

5. Leaders make unexpected connections (you see patterns that lead to small innovations and breakthrough ideas).

6. Leaders provide direction (you give direction, not answers; you are in touch and out front).

7. Leaders protect their people from danger, and they expose them to reality (you don't insulate your people from change; you mobilize them to face it).

8. Leaders make change and stand for values that don't change (you know what habits and assumptions need to be changed and the values that need to be maintained).

9. Leaders lead by example (small gestures send big messages, and you live by principle).

10. Leaders don't blame: They learn (you try, fail, learn, and try again).
11. Leaders look for and network with other leaders (it's only lonely at the top if you place yourself on a pedestal).
12. The job of leader: Make more leaders (you know this is your ultimate job).

You may never find one leader who exhibits all of these qualities, but if you do, please send me his or her phone number so I can apply for a job. On second thought, I already know of one: Sir Richard Branson. He takes all of the above steps to visionary leadership and goes one trait further: He adds a remarkable sense of humor and a unique ability to show he does not take himself too seriously. This happy, grinning Englishman has run a virtual empire of Virgin brands on which the sun has never set. They go from windmills to condoms—they're called "Mates"—from financial products to railways; from retail stores to property management; from entertainment to publishing. His hit list of potential Virgins is absolutely endless. A fun-loving version of Ralph Nader with an eccentric John Cleese twist, he earned a reputation as the people's crusader with brands that are different or better, fun, less expensive, or more comfortable. Every time he goes forth to conquer, the public cheers him on. If you think this is a reputational exaggeration, remember British youth chose him over Mother Teresa as their most likely choice to rewrite The Ten Commandments.

Branson loves being different. His first foray into business offered young people a new way to buy music through the mail. When a postal strike nearly sank the business, he quickly opened music stores with a social difference from anything England's young people had ever seen: stores where you could hang out, lounge around on beanbags with friends, and stay as long as you wanted. He did these things at an age when most of us were still in high school!

For years, Branson operated his corporate offices out of a houseboat that he also lived in with his wife and children. He only moved out of it when she finally put her foot down about living in a madhouse. Even today he has a loathing for formal offices. When I first wrote about him in my previous book, his staff of 20,000+ not working in his stores or airplanes were in a multitude of odd houses all over the map. At that time, his corporate headquarters had fewer than 20 people in a house in London. He practices the opposite of command and control.

Each Virgin Company is its own small unit. When a company gets bigger than 60 people, he splits off a new one and appoints new management from within the ranks to run yet another company. The new people make their own decisions and get on with them. Managers get a share of the businesses they run.

Branson once put out a bet that he would ski down a Swiss mountain stark naked. When nobody took the bet, he did it anyway. His derring-do in balloon flight is legend and once nearly cost him his life. He is the leader we all want to be when we don't grow up. He proves the leader sets the tone, along with the operational ethic, and that we are attracted to brands that are different, even a little quirky. Eccentricity in the brand leader can make the brand feel charming and approachable, and it makes us smile a smile of recognition.

My own vision of leadership may not be as quirky, but it is different from what you might read in leadership manuals. I liken it to the work of the gandy dancer, a title that hearkens back to the glory days of the railroad. Gandy dancing describes workers who walked the rails with a sledgehammer in hand to keep the rails straight and parallel. The powerful locomotives would not have made it far without the watchful eye of the gandy dancer, working on point, keeping things straight with the destination always in mind. A visionary, gandy-dancing leader understands when you take care of the tracks, the trains will take care of themselves.

The words come from another time, but there was prophecy in what President John F. Kennedy said with so much eloquence in his inaugural address: "It is time for a new generation of leadership to cope with new problems and new opportunities. For there is a new world to be won."

CHAPTER 9

The Employee Is the Brand

●　●　●

KNOWLTON, A PRETTY VICTORIAN VILLAGE ABOUT AN hour's drive from Montreal in Quebec's Eastern Townships, sits on Lac-Brome, surrounded by ski slopes nestled into the encompassing mountains. With its sleepy bucolic setting and a population of around 5,000, it is hardly a hotbed of entrepreneurial zeal, which is why it is surprising to find somebody like the genial Paul Côté running a successful international business there.

Côté is founder and CEO of Brome Bird Care, which is headquartered in a modest house on the village's main street. The company, now 13 years old, was born out of Côté's personal frustration with squirrels. Unable to keep the pesky critters from stealing the seed from his birdfeeder, he said "enough is enough" and invented a new kind of feeder. He actually cobbled a rough prototype right in his own basement workshop and christened it the Squirrel Buster. It works with an ingenious but simple spring pressure mechanism that controls access to the feeder so that critters like squirrels can't get at the seeds, which drives them crazy. The spring can be adjusted to a bird's weight to allow access only to small birds and reject the big greedy guys like blue jays, who hog almost as much seed as the squirrels. From this extremely humble beginning in his basement, Paul created a highly successful business organized to sell his one-of-a-kind birdfeeders in Canada, the U.S., and 13 other countries in Europe's economic union. The Squirrel Buster is the largest-selling birdfeeder on Amazon. Product costs are kept down by manufacturing through suppliers in China. Business growth has been 10 percent a year and is expected to go beyond that in the next five years.

While growth is impressive, what is even more so is how Paul readily grasps the concepts of branding with all the finesse of a Harvard MBA grad leading a huge multinational brand. His business savvy embodies the enlightened sentiments of business guru Peter Drucker, who said, "…[T]he modern business enterprise is a human and social organization. Management as a discipline and as a practice deals with human social values… [O]nly when management succeeds in making the human resources of the organization productive is it able to maintain the desired outside objectives and results."

Paul is the kind of leader Thomas Petzinger Jr. described in his book *The New Pioneers*, one who has freed himself from the straightjacket of what he calls "Newtonianism," a mechanistic view of business that says output is exactly proportional to input, that management is an act of calibration and control, and that the whole is always equal to the sum of the parts.

Like a growing number of enlightened executives, Côté understands that the process of taking things apart (analysis) is not nearly so intellectually profitable as putting them together (synthesis), and thinking in terms of systems rather than one-way causality gives a better view of what Petzinger calls "the big picture." Côté then points out the new pioneers entering management from the ranks of the Baby Boomers "also had an inkling that 'happiness and fulfillment in the workplace might actually devolve to the benefit of the organization itself; indeed, in surveying their employees, MCI, Sears, and other giants found a significant link between morale and revenue. What a concept: Treating people individually and with dignity—the [tenet] of virtually every religion in the history of the planet—turns out to be good for business!" And I would add that the question "How does it make you feel?" is a good question not only for customers but also for employees and other stakeholders.

Coté starts any conversation of his business with the statement that it is "staff-driven." He says, "Nothing makes more sense to me than the fact that you cannot have a great brand without passionate and motivated people to run it and represent it. They are the face and heart of any business where it really counts—with suppliers and customers. If you get that right, all other things being equal, you get the business right."

Coté's choice of people starts with a unique recruitment process: Living in a small community, he gets to know and observe people as they go about their daily lives, and he makes a mental note of those who impress him with their willingness to take on responsibility not just in their work but in their personal lives. He goes with the idea that skills can be taught, but character is what really counts. The president of the company was formerly the receptionist at the town hall. The most recent hire was his dentist's office secretary, who is now the customer care manager. And all the employees could even have known each other before they went to work for the company. As you walk around the offices to chat with the eight employees, you get the feeling it's a family business in the truest sense of the word, and indeed, one of Paul's mantras is "family comes first." An employee with a sick child is expected to put as much time into caring for the child as the child requires without the employee worrying about time off work. Other employees take over his or her job—it's a common practice that the others will cook and deliver food and provide taxi service if needed. Six months after she was hired, the latest employee discovered she was pregnant. Paul was delighted to hear the news and threw a party to celebrate the company's first birth. She also got all the time needed to come back to work after the birth. And when one employee went into the hospital for surgery, the company hired a maid to keep her house clean. The list of personal attentions goes on and on, but more formalized benefits are just as impressive.

Every employee gets a free iPad, plus a free smart phone, including service. Additionally, Côté's people get free medical insurance to cover costs outside of Quebec's government-run program, such as dental, prescription, and eyeglasses. They're also given free membership to the gym of their choice. And, remarkably, every winter, all employees get a free week's vacation in the Caribbean at an all-inclusive resort of their choice! Out of a $600,000 a year payroll, Paul assigns as much money as he can to employee benefits, which he says is worth every cent to cultivate the well-being of what he calls the company's most important asset.

All this staff care leads to exemplary care for the brand's customers. As Paul says, the objective is to "blow customers' socks off" with personal attention that begins with a nice person answering the phone. He says, "We have a standout product line with a 100 percent blanket guarantee and a constant product improvement effort in our separate research facility, but it is all for naught if you do not pay very close attention to what your customers have to say. We actually want to hear from them, and in particular when it is a complaint; in fact, fixing problems right away and in person with good cheer is what has made many of our customers our most prolific brand advocates. With them on our side spreading the word for us we find very little need for consumer advertising." The same is true for the small army of independent dealers he services through a cadre of select distributors. Paul adds, "They are also our customers and deserve the same care and attention as our end users. We think of them as what they are: an essential and integral part of the brand's marketing effort. We go out of our way to do things for them that other manufacturers do not."

An important fact of the matter is Brome Bird Care has zero employee turnover, which in the long run cuts out the trouble and expense of hiring and training. You might be thinking it is relatively easy for such a small company to accomplish these human resource feats, but the new pioneers are now also running huge companies that follow a similar philosophy. They, too, go against the grain of requiring crippling work hours and stupefying stress. *Fast Company's* Charles Fishman says the SAS Institute near Raleigh, North Carolina, is "the sanest company in North America." It produces very expensive software that makes it possible to sift through mountains of information to find pattern and meaning. With sales of $750 million, the company employs 5,400 people worldwide. But huge success isn't the only thing that separates SAS from other high-tech enterprises; the other is fanatically devoted employees.

Fishman continues, "In an age of relentless pressure this place is an oasis of calm. In an age of frantic competition this place is methodical and clear-headed. In a world of free agency, signing bonuses, and stock options, here's a place where loyalty matters more than money."

People leave the office by 5 P.M., after a seven-hour workday, but you may find them in the company's 36,000 square feet of gym space at 6 A.M. Or they're getting a massage, taking classes in golf, African dance, tennis, and Tai chi. You might see them dropping off their kids at the company daycare center. The company even launders and returns employees' workout clothes with next-day service. CEO Jim Goodnight shows us that there is profit in benevolence. His actions are a far cry from some tech companies' idea of flextime and letting people name their own hours—any 18 hours a day they like. Or how about the Chiat Day ad agency that said, "Of course you can take Sunday off, but if you do, don't bother coming in on Monday."? This attitude earned the company the nickname Chiat Day and Night.

In these kinds of organizations, people are afraid to assume normal hours for fear they will look like slackers. The old ideas of command and control leadership are also a lot less fun for the boss during his workday. If, like Paul Côté, you think the goal is to make every employee his or her own boss, you also make them as responsible as you are for your company's success. Asked where he learned this stuff, he responds, "My dream was to build a happy company, to see it working. I learned what not to do from 30 years in the rat race."

Chapter 9: The Employee Is the Brand

Even factory work is more collaborative these days, and certainly our fathers must shake their heads in wonder at the state of the contemporary workplace. In Silicon Valley, where attracting and keeping brainpower is paramount, it seems people do not work in "offices." They work in fully contained "campuses" laden with unprecedented perks. Apple's "Spaceship Headquarters," on a 70-hectare campus, includes an orchard for engineers to wander around in. Facebook's Disney-inspired campus has a Main Street with a barbecue shack, a sushi house, and a bike shop. In many work environments it is not usual to have espresso bars; lessons in cardio and kick-boxing; walls you can draw on; golf classes, child care, a climbing wall, a bowling alley, banks, gyms, laundry facilities, and employees' dogs. When you go to the Skywalker Ranch, set up by George Lucas himself, you work in what can look like a winery or a Victorian mansion in a spacious park-like setting in California's golden hills on the Berkeley side of the San Francisco Bay. These are all quite wonderful—to say nothing of very expensive—ways to make employees feel valued and crucially important.

Out of all the leadership stories of employee empowerment I could quote in this book, my favorite has to be one from the U.S. Navy. Military service—it may strike you as a classic environment for top-down command and control leadership of the most archaic kind. Unfailing obedience is a necessity for men and women required to put their lives on the line. Serving in the military would hardly seem to include the listening and questioning model the digital age's enlightened leadership requires. Doing things by the book is *de rigueur*. It's shape up or ship out. If it moves, salute it; if it doesn't move, paint it. Ours is not to reason why; ours is but to do or die. There's the right way, the wrong way, and the Navy way. No questions asked as you go over the top, boys and girls. Remember that it's not too many years ago that sailors were pressed into service—literally kidnapped and hauled aboard to serve what must have felt like a criminal sentence, as they were tied to the rigging and flogged with a cat-o'-nine-tails for minor rule infractions. It's hardly the ideal environment for what Peter Drucker calls "systematic innovation."

That's what is so impressive about the story of the captain of the *USS Benfold*—a formidable $1 billion warship armed with the world's most advanced and lethal computer-controlled combat system. Fast Company's Polly LaBarre reported that the *Benfold*'s Commander, D. Michael Abrashoff, is a model of leadership that is as progressive as any in the business world, but for me, it's because he's in the military that I think the commander's story is even more astonishing.

The 28-year-old Abrashoff had a sterling service record, including combat experience; but it's his ship and her crew that he talks about with unabashed pride. When he took command, the *Benfold* was classified as one of the worst ships in the Navy. Under his transforming leadership, the ship was ultimately credited with having the best record in the Pacific fleet for combat readiness. To keep it that way, he saw his mission as "nothing less than the reorientation of a famously rigid 200-year-old hierarchy." His aim: To focus on purpose rather than on chain of command:

> "When you shift your organizing principle from obedience to performance, the highest boss is no longer the guy with the most stripes—it's the sailor who does the work. There's nothing magical about it… In most organizations today, ideas still come from the top. Soon after arriving at this command, I realized that the young folks on this ship are smart and talented. And I realized that my job was to listen aggressively—to pick up all of the ideas that they had for improving how we operate."

Abrashoff truly believes "the most important thing a captain can do is to see the ship from the eyes of her crew." Believing there's always a better way to do things, he probed those better ways in great detail with the crew. He and his men dissected every operation to see how each one helped the crew to maintain operational readiness. There was no reticence about making some stunning changes that seem highly unusual for a military organization. Anything and everything that was done just because "that's the way we always do things" was jettisoned overboard. In his mission to create true operational readiness, Abrashoff pursued a policy of what Peter F. Drucker has called "Organizational Abandonment."

Many of his superiors and fellow commanding officers questioned Abrashoff's methods. He says, "I divide the world into believers and infidels. What the infidels don't understand—and they far outnumber the believers—is that innovative practices combined with true empowerment produce phenomenal results."

One of Abrashoff's confident insights into change is the more people enjoy the process, the better the results. Spending 35 days in the Persian Gulf is no fun for a crew of very young people, but during replenishment alongside supply ships, the *Benfold's* crews are known throughout the region for projecting music videos on the ship's side. In purchasing food for the ship, Abrashoff switched from high-cost naval provisions to cheaper, better-quality, name-brand foods. With the money he saved, he sent five of the *Benfold*'s 13 cooks to cooking school, which made the *Benfold* a favorite lunchtime destination for crews across the San Diego waterfront. Abrashoff's ship had a $2.4 million maintenance budget and a $3 million repair budget. He was able to return $1.4 million of these amounts to the Navy's top line, which he credits to a proactive environment in which people simply want to do well.

On average, only 54 percent of sailors remain in the Navy after their second tour of duty. Under Abrashoff's command, 100 percent of the *Benfold*'s career sailors signed on for another tour. Abrashoff figures this saved $1.6 million in costs related to personnel. He understood scraping and chipping paint was a hated chore and a waste of younger crewmen's time and talent, so he farmed the job out and incalculably boosted morale, while increasing the young sailors' time for training and combat readiness; doing so also got the ship a paint job that lasts 30 years for a mere $25,000. On his watch, the *Benfold*'s sailors came out winners in the advancement cycle, with promotions twice as high as the Navy average. Abrashoff created an Internet account so the sailors on sea duty can send and get messages home daily through a commercial satellite. When new crewmen arrived fresh from boot camp, they were greeted with a welcome plan, which included a handpicked mentor and the right to call home (on Abrashoff's nickel) to let the folks know they had arrived safely. He made sure he knew every crewman through face-to-face meetings and understood his or her goals. Needless to say, he remembered every person's name.

When Abrashoff learned that credit card debt was causing serious trouble for many of the young crew, he hired financial consultants to give the needed advice. He broadcast new ideas over the ship's loudspeakers. Sailors made a suggestion one week and saw it implemented the next. According to Abrashoff, there was a balance in his approach:

> "None of this means we sacrificed discipline or cohesion on the ship. When I walked down the passageway, people called attention on deck and hit the bulkhead. They respected the office but understood I don't care about the fluff: I want substance, and the substance is combat readiness. The substance is having people feel good about what they do. The substance is treating

people with respect and dignity. We gain a lot of ground by keeping our focus on substance rather than a lot of extraneous stuff."

The examples and sterling results of Abrashoff's intense-listening command style go on and on. They would indeed create envy in the best leaders in business today. He says, "In many units—and in many businesses—a lot of time and effort is spent supporting the guy on top. Anyone on my ship will tell you that I'm a low-maintenance CO. It's not about me; it's about my crew."

Abrashoff reveals his six principles that made the *Benfold* a working example of great grassroots leadership:

1. Don't just take command; communicate purpose.
2. Leaders listen without prejudice.
3. Practice discipline without formalism.
4. The best captains hand out responsibility, not orders.
5. Successful crews perform with devotion.
6. True change is permanent: once you start perestroika, you can't really stop it.

I would like to see these principles engraved in stone and hung on the wall of every CEO's office. If no other leadership principles were presented in this or any other book, Commander Abrashoff's would be enough.

Abrashoff also says, "I'm lucky. All I ever wanted to do in the Navy was to command a ship. I don't care if I ever got promoted again. And that attitude has enabled me to do the right things for my people instead of doing the right things for my career. In the process I ended up with the best ship in the Navy—and I got the best evaluation of my career." After completing his 20-month tour of duty on the *Benfold*, Commander Abrashoff reported to a top post at the Space and Naval Warfare Systems Command. He has since left the Navy and successfully writes and lectures on the subject of leadership.

The lesson in empowerment is one of leadership's primary goals. You don't hire people so you can tell them what to do: You hire people so you never have to tell them what to do. Leadership is what happens when you are not there. As the leader, you are needed for keeping the faith, making final decisions, providing direction in emergencies, and plotting your brand's future. You might also be needed for playing the trombone in the company band. It's a good idea to remind yourself that you are not Stalin and your company isn't Russia. When you enter the boardroom, you do not have to change from the personal "you" to the corporate "you." Very simply, people want to work for, and do business with, those they can respect and admire who espouse leadership from carefully constructed principles and values.

Leaders get it very right when they absorb the beautifully expressed advice of American social worker Mary Parker Follett, an organizational theory and organizational management pioneer, who wrote the following way back in 1918:

> "The leader guides the group and is at the same time guided by the group, is always part of the group... Authority, genuine authority, is the outcome of our common life. It does not come from separating people, from dividing them into two classes: those who command and those who obey. It comes from the intermingling of all, of my work fitting into yours and yours into mine."

CHAPTER 10

Brand You

● ● ●

THE FIRST TIME I SAW AN ARTICLE IN THE MAGAZINE *Fast Company* about how individuals might think of themselves as brands, I felt a little repulsed. I didn't like the idea of thinking of myself, or anybody else, as a package of attributes to be marketed or dialed up and down like public sentiment in a political poll. But the article was by *Fast Company's* insightful thought leader, Tom Peters, and I felt compelled to read it. Since then, I've seen the idea in several other publications, and I've tried it on for size.

I discovered it could be a useful tool for raising one's self-awareness, for consciously thinking of your own behavior. It's a little like what I wrote earlier about being mindful. If you can adopt within yourself the lessons in this book and apply them to the daily journey of interactions in your personal and business life, it's a little like living with an internal philosopher in the true meaning of the word, which in my definition is one who sheds light on ways to be.

It occurs to me that Brand You might make a good course for high school and college students and certainly business schools. After all, it's basically about learning how to be a responsible, more effective individual. But because it takes a very personal tack, it might be a more quirky way to reach kids on such grim topics—at least in their eyes—as everyday morals and ethics. The text takes an abstract and makes it personal, like listening to the highly palatable advice of a motivational speaker, e.g., Betty Binder, who says things like, "When people go to work, they shouldn't have to leave their hearts at home," which is more personally involving than passively saying "be natural."

However, Brand You also works best with people who don't need to be reminded that life is best lived with a nonrefundable sense of humor. As long as you understand a brand starts with all the trust of a handshake, you're fine. If you want to communicate that you are the person who will do what you say you will do when you say you will do it, being a brand can help you maintain that focus. But to keep your brand from becoming handcuffed to an unreasonable standard and taking it all too seriously, Brand You must resolve to enjoy doing what you say, not just for other people but for its own sake. It's not a movement or a religion; it just feels good. Remember effective behavior is something most adults do without their ever having heard of self-branding.

The idea is to become the CEO of Brand You. If you have a job, your boss is your customer and Brand You is the supplier of services. Your wages become your sales, and it's easy to see how your brand puts a new perspective on how you perform and conduct yourself—in your present and certainly your future, probably one of your vital interests, one that Brand You might try not to leave to the casual blowing of the wind.

Branding yourself will help you resolve to sharpen and resharpen your skills and to always acquire new ones. You will think beyond the financial transaction of your job. You will work at creating value in your relationships with others—from the person at the reception desk to the one in the back room who prepares your paycheck, i.e., you will be the kind of person you would like to hire or the boss you would like to work for because loyalty is far more fundamental than self-interest.

There used to be more loyalty between companies and their employees in the days before the adoption of the euphemism we know as "downsizing." In the days when people actually pursued a one-company career, there was a premium placed on climbing the ladder. You found something you were good at and exploited it in one place.

Nowadays, as Tom Peters says, you might think of yourself differently. You're not an employee or a staffer. You don't belong to any company for life, and your chief affiliation isn't to any particular function. You're not defined by your job title, and you're not confined by your job description; rather, says Peters, loyalty is still alive and well, but it is loyalty to your project, your team, your customers, and yourself. "We are the CEOs of our own companies: Me Inc. To be in business today, our most important job is to be head marketer for the brand called You."

Peters continues: "...[T]he main chance is becoming a free agent in an economy of free agents, looking to have the best season you can imagine in your field, looking to do your best work and chalk up a remarkable track record, and looking to establish your own micro equivalent of the Nike swoosh."

Considering the fraying bond between employers and employees, it's not bad advice. Major corporations issue more than 3 million pink slips annually. Considering job searches usually last a month for every $10,000 of a person's salary, you're looking at a lot of sorely missed paydays. Employment statistics point to a shortage of really well-qualified help, but it doesn't seem to quell the canning of huge numbers of people.

What's surprising is that Wall Street interprets downsizing not as a source of potential trouble for a company in the market place but a sign of greater efficiency. Companies that feel compelled to fire thousands are often rewarded with a higher stock price for their supposed prudence in getting rid of bloat. You would think allowing bloat to occur in the first place would be a sign of poor management or of irresponsible management not paying attention to the preservation of the brand's assets.

In forming Brand You, Peters suggests intense self-examination and the writing of a statement that starts with answering the question, "What is it that my product or service does that makes it different?" in 15 words or fewer. The answer should light up the eyes of a prospective employer.

I once playfully wrote what I thought would be Jack's mission statement: "Nobody enjoys working as hard as I do to deliver consistently effective creative work." When I showed these 14 words to him, he crossed them out and wrote: "My work will never fail to make you happy." Jack then wrote what he thought would be my mission statement: "Leadership from ingrained integrity; results from great expectations." I told him flattery would get him everywhere, except in line for a bonus.

You can create visibility for Brand You by writing articles for magazines that are devoured by other people in your field. You can start an online, idea-sharing club to extend your network influence, even on LinkedIn. You can take on freelance projects to enhance your repertoire of skills and make new contacts. You can offer to speak, as long as you have a good speech that will either illuminate our minds or leave us weak-kneed with laughter.

Of course, you can conduct yourself in every one of your dealings as a person who will stand up to be counted with great gusto and good cheer every day of your life. The latter is probably as good a way to succeed as any. As an employer, I can tell you that skilled, positive, decent people with high emotional intelligence are worth their weight in gold, whether they think of themselves as brands or not. As Albert Einstein said, "Try not to become a man of success but a man of value." As I say, "Work to become, not to beget."

In *Fast Company*, Tom Peters said, "In the new economy, all work is project work, and you can make them all go 'Wow!' You can use projects to show your value, to leave a legacy, or to make yourself a star. Project work is the vehicle by which the powerless gain power... Somewhere, in the belly of every company, someone is working away in obscurity on the project that 10 years from now everyone will acknowledge as the company's proudest moment."

Peters suggests that you "volunteer for every lousy project that comes along: Organize the office Christmas party. (Turn that dreadful holiday party into an event that says 'Thanks for a terrific year' to all employees.)"

Never let a project go dreary on you. Use the project to create surprising new ways of looking at old problems. No project is too mundane to become a "Wow!" project if you attack it with passion and recruit "Wow!" people to help you with it. Everything is a golden learning opportunity if you keep your eyes and ears open. Five criteria for judging each project are: Wow! Beautiful! Revolutionary! Impact! Raving Fans!

Peters gives an example of turning a dull chore assignment, e.g., cleaning up the warehouse, into a "Wow!" project: You see quickly what looks like a messy warehouse is really a poorly organized warehouse. This involves necessarily both incoming parts for suppliers and outgoing parts to customers, which in turn makes the case for a new distribution system that would feed flawlessly into a newly reorganized warehouse that will now stay neat because of newly designed processes that fit the new distribution system perfectly.

In *The 7 Habits of Highly Effective People and Principle-Centered Leadership,* Stephen Covey puts forward the idea that leadership is not equated with any kind of position. We have bought into this top-down control model, but we can ignore it if we choose. Covey says you can become your own pilot program for leadership from the position you now occupy. Just think back to Commander Abrashoff and what he did with slim but eager resources.

Assume responsibility. Be proactive. Flex your boss muscle. Exceed your authority. As Jack says, "It is better to ask for forgiveness than for permission." If you want to be the boss, start by assuming you already are. If the barriers are too great for your future development, think about your alternatives. Covey says, "Never let your professional development be governed by your company. People without options are running scared. They tend to become reactive. When you have alternatives of employment, you don't have to be angry, whine, or moan; you just go somewhere else."

This advice is particularly sage if your boss is a control freak or thinks of you as nothing more than a profit center and a contributor to his personal pension fund. You might not always be able to change the world, but you can always change your job.

One author suggests you should take a good look at your name and change it if it represents a negative image. It's there that I draw the line. A rose wouldn't smell as sweet by any other name, and neither would you. If your name is Eddie Schmuck (we know one), I think you should wear it proudly. Let the rabble with ordinary names snigger at your moniker as you leave them in the dust with your competence and good cheer.

Remember, it was an Englishman named Crapper who invented the flush toilet—thus, the nickname for the commode. Without any concern for a Germanic name that doesn't exactly tinkle in the ear like an angel's bells, it's a guy named Schwab who practically invented the online brokerage business. There is a lot in a name but even more in what you make out of it. Who in their right mind would name a company Yahoo!, Zappos, or even Apple? The guys who want to stand out, who want to say we're way beyond ordinary, who want to announce a new kind of iconoclastic force—that's who!

It's a lot more interesting and involving than the "Generals" of the 19th and early 20th century: General Electric, General Dynamics, General Motors, General Telephone and Electronics, etc. Come to think of it, a funnier name would be General Yahoo!

As Jack says, however, "You might want to rethink the name Hitler. Having the name Hitler is as nasty as chewing tobacco and the amazing amount of spitting that goes along with it. There's nothing funny about it. It has no socially redeemable qualities. It's not going to get you any kind of leverage for a first date. And it's obviously bad for the state of your longevity. If my name were Hitler, I'd change it to Montana. I love the name Montana; in fact, I'd change both names. There's something not quite right about Adolf Montana."

Jack might also have changed his name if he wanted to go into the fashion business with a name like Ralph Lifshitz. He would have changed it to Ralph Lauren. But Jack does not condone a crazy name just for the sake of craziness. He says he would never have called a shoe company Zappos simply because the word has nothing to do with shoes: "I would have called it Feets, or Footsies, or Hop Alongs. A name like *Twitter* is brilliant because it instantly tells what the product is with wit and curious intelligence, but what in the world is a Zappo?"

In *Management Challenges for the 21st Century*, Peter Drucker takes the hype out of making yourself a brand by simply calling it, "Managing Oneself." With the rise of the "knowledge worker," he says it's more and more crucial for career longevity. Drucker says you don't plan careers: You prepare for them, and you do so by searching out the answers to three critical questions:

1. What are my strengths?
2. How do I perform?
3. What are my values?

All three questions are important, but I find "How do I perform?" to be the most illuminating. Drucker gives us an extraordinary insight when he says most people perform by either reading or listening, so it is imperative you know which way you perform.

During World War II, Allied commander General Dwight Eisenhower was always sharp as a tack at press briefings. All questions were answered thoroughly and in beautifully polished sentences. When he became president, however, he was terrible in front of the press and with its questions. He rambled, was often incoherent, and became a laughingstock for bumbling speech.

The difference between the two situations can be found in the fact Eisenhower was a reader, not a listener. During the war, he insisted all questions be submitted to him in writing prior to a press briefing. This allowed him to read everything before he prepared his response, which he probably wrote. In Washington, however, he had no such luxury. He had to respond on the spot after simply listening to press questions, and he found it very difficult.

By contrast, President Lyndon Johnson was primarily a listener. Drucker says one of the reasons Johnson destroyed his presidency is he didn't know he was a listener. He thought he had to do the same as his predecessor, John Kennedy, who was a reader. Johnson had to absorb everything from written reports. We're talking about reports from brilliant writers, like Arthur Schlesinger Jr. and Bill Moyers, but he apparently never got one word of what they wrote, simply because he didn't know he learned by listening, not reading. You've heard the expression "He's good on his feet." When I hear that, I know the subject is somebody who is a listener—and probably a talker—not primarily a reader or a writer.

Most writers perform and learn by writing rather than by reading or listening. Jack says he can't go to the bathroom without a pen in his hand. He says, "I write; therefore, I think." Writers often don't do well in school and find it torture—like Winston Churchill—because they are required to learn by listening and reading rather than writing. This insight leads one to wonder about an entire educational system that imparts knowledge via teachers talking to a class full of students, regardless of each individual's learning predilection. It certainly favors the listeners.

Many people actually learn by talking. You can almost hear their brain-frames processing as they verbalize what's going on in their noggins. A lot of college professors say, from talking out a subject in the classroom, they learn what they want to write for publication. Still others learn by doing, so you can see how important it is to know how you learn and perform so that you don't make the mistake of putting a value on one method over the other.

It is important to know not only how *you* perform but also how *the people around you* perform. If your boss learns by listening, don't make her life difficult by writing everything. A listener-boss might say, "I want that report on my desk by

Monday morning," but do not make the mistake of just writing it. Make sure you get the chance to tell it. Of course, if the boss is a reader, don't waste her time, or incur her wrath, by doing everything verbally.

As Drucker says, "In all your dealings, you have to assume relationship responsibility *as a duty*. This includes the simple but effective idea that good manners go a long way to helping you get good results." Drucker adds, "Bright people—especially bright young people—often do not understand that manners are the 'lubricating oil' of an organization."

With more than manners in mind, you are bound to meet people you have to struggle to get along with. This is hardly a very good reason for Brand You to deprecate their intelligence. You might think someone dumb because they don't agree with your point of view, but the state of another's intellect is often not the issue, i.e., the dumb one is unlikely to see himself in an unfavorable light, but the degree of his dumbness probably goes up with the degree of your frustration. If you really think he is dumb, the natural conclusion is you are the smart one. If you are indeed the superior intellect, you presumably have the brainy wherewithal to persuade him to understand your point of view!

You have to take responsibility for figuring out how associates perform, learn, and communicate so that you can work better with them. Ask them to tell you their preferences, and they will appreciate it.

You don't have to like all the people in your working life, but it is helpful to respect and even trust them. They will feel it if you do. Nine times out of ten, they will respond in kind. As you take responsibility for your relationships, it's amazing how simple manners can pave the way. Perhaps lessons in branding should start with the reading of Emily Post. And never believe anybody who says, "I don't care what people think of me." Only hermits and psychopaths can say that with real conviction. You do not have to worry about everybody's opinion of you. However, certainly our social natures seek the approval of our peers and those in authority. It probably starts in childhood, when we want to get our way with our fathers, mothers and siblings—it goes from there with a desire to have people think well of us in general. You might be able to rise through life's ranks with no concern for others, but it is unlikely you will stay anywhere near the top for long—if indeed that is where you want to be.

In the end, you have to write your own story. George Bernard Shaw said, "This is the true joy in life, the being used for a purpose recognized by yourself as a mighty one...being a force of nature instead of a feverish, selfish little clod of ailments and grievances complaining that the world will not devote itself to making you happy."

CHAPTER 11

The Starting Gate

●　●　●

A BOOK LIKE THIS CAN MOTIVATE YOU TO DO something. It can make you feel as though the way you manage your career or your business is hardly good enough—the time has come for some big moves. It can generate a deep desire to become a broom of sweeping change.

If the book is as motivating as I would like it to be, you may even feel something akin to an epiphany. You're going to march into the office tomorrow morning with every intention of shaking the tree to its very roots. You're going to demand initiative.

Well, hold your horses.

The problem is that this is not a motivational diet book that promises a new, radiantly skinny you in 10 short days. It's not a serendipitous idea you pick up from a self-help guru that will transform your life with a new vision. It's a business book intended to offer you some ideas that could help you do a better, more profitable and satisfying job for yourself and all your stakeholders. But please go slowly! The Digital Age may travel at the speed of light, but you can approach your new, improved brand at a more human pace. While it's good to feel motivated, it's wise to stop once in a while to ask of your progress, "How does it make me feel?" More importantly, "How do the changes I propose benefit my customers?"

Start with yourself. What obvious personal strengths do you feel as a result of reading this book? Obvious weaknesses? Most important of all, what can you do to change in small, incremental ways?

If you want to be really gutsy, ask your colleagues to evaluate you and to suggest three changes they would like to see you make in yourself. If they suggest you could achieve the ultimate self-improvement by replacing yourself, you are in deep trouble! Ask some trusted customers and suppliers to evaluate your performance and that of your company. After absorbing all of this information, make one change a week, using Commander D. Michael Abrashoff as a leadership role model. He didn't make the changes on his ship: He was merely the catalyst; his crew made the changes. He knows people tend to resist change, but they embrace it when they instigate it. Asking them for their opinions, questions, and answers will mightily motivate them. Giving them the power to do what they see has to be done is immeasurably effective. It says volumes about you and your style of leadership and how you want your company and its brands to be perceived.

You might feel uncomfortable in the world of social media, but getting a handle on it is crucial. Start by reading *Wikibrands*; then enlist some IT people to guide you. Maybe your ad agency has a dedicated social media division you can tap into. If it doesn't, find one that does.

In his book *Direct from Dell*, Dell Inc. Founder and CEO Michael Dell says, "It's easy to fall in love with how far you've come and how much you've done. It's definitely harder to see the cracks in a structure you've built yourself, but that's all the more reason to look hard and look often. Even if something seems to be working, it can be improved."

Talk with your staff. Get them talking to each other. If you have departments, start with one of them and share questions about a few little things that might lead to improvements in the way you do business. For example, ask each member of the department to share three suggestions that will improve how they do business with customers. Stimulate them with the idea you believe it's much more important to develop relationships than just transactions. Instill the attitude that getting credit doesn't matter as much as getting results, that it's their company and their future that's at stake.

Get them all talking. In the chapter entitled "Nobody's as Smart as Everybody," in his book *The New Pioneers*, Thomas Petzinger wrote about groups of minds:

> "Will they explore a wider, more creative space through social interaction or through outside command? Though the answer should be obvious, consider the case of the heart surgeons from five hospitals in New England who spent 1996 observing each other's practices and talking about their work. The result was a stunning 24 percent decline in mortality rates in bypass surgery, the equivalent of seventy-four saved lives, a result they could never have obtained through the traditional continuing educational regimen of listening to lectures, reading articles, or even logging into artificial 'knowledge management' systems...as one biologist quips, 'I link, therefore I am.'"

If you think only professionals can get results through the simple, human process of comparing notes, go back and read about Commander Abrashoff's accomplishments with young, wet-behind-the-ears high-school graduates. I bet he doesn't have many PhDs on his payroll.

Another idea is to start a dialogue on the broader discussion of how to develop a higher calling. Don't just do this with your most-senior colleagues: Start at the grass roots. You might be surprised at how interested your whole team might be in getting beyond just working for wages. Read other books on the subject of branding and creative leadership, but remember the advice of Peter Senge: "Your company isn't a machine that can be fixed by a mechanic; it's a living organism that needs gardeners to keep it healthy and growing. Don't just change it; cultivate it, and remember that everything in a garden starts by being small. Senge's garden analogy reminds me of the Buddhist expression that when you want a tree to grow, you don't water the leaves; you water the roots."

Peter Drucker said, "Success does not require special gifts, special aptitude, or special training. Effectiveness as an executive demands doing certain—and fairly simple—things. It consists of a small number of practices."

Obviously, small steps can come from inside your organization, but they can include forming alliances with other companies as a way to learn. You can also make a small acquisition or form a joint venture for modest expansion before you bet the farm on big changes. Pilot everything of importance. Piloting helps you to learn the positives and negatives from making small changes so you can be a lot smarter about making big ones.

A lot of this stuff is basic. Senge says most people would rather work with a group of people who trust one another. Our decisions are driven by emotion, how we feel in a given situation.

Most people would rather walk out of a meeting with the belief they've just solved an important problem. Most people would rather have fun at work. It may be obvious, but we've observed consistently that personal enthusiasm is the initial energizer of any change process. That enthusiasm feeds on itself. People don't necessarily want to "have a vision" at work or to "conduct a dialogue." They want to be part of a fun-to-work-with team that produces results they are proud of.

These are all conditions you can lead and manage. The point is we shouldn't get caught up in the jargon of corporate change; change is useless until it helps people do their jobs better for their own and their customers' satisfaction. People feel—and are—truly important when they get a sense of how valuable their contribution can be.

That's the secret of Commander Abrashoff's having the best ship with an elite crew in the whole Pacific fleet. It's why Richard Branson has such a huge employee and customer following for his Virgin brands. It could be the secret for your having the best brands in the best company in the market in which you want to be best!

While change may be necessary and worthwhile, it's axiomatic that all change is disruptive. Both good and bad changes take a similar emotional toll on a person's system. It's the same for brands. It might be necessary, for a while, to make friends with ambiguity and paradox, as they are the best pals of creativity, but just be sure you get the intended result when you initiate change. Don't let change bite the hand that feeds it.

Alexander Rose wrote the following in the *Financial Post*:

"In the time of Socrates, the Delphic Oracle was considered the center of the Earth. Greeks would travel to the Oracle to ask questions of the gods and receive a reply, which unfortunately took the form of an amphiboly (a statement whose meaning is indeterminate in a peculiar way). Thus, in 559 BC, the fabulously wealthy King Croesus of Lydia asked the Oracle whether he should wage war against Persia and was told that if he did so he would destroy a great kingdom. Taking this as a yes, King Croesus attacked the Persians under Cyrus the Great, but lost the war and destroyed his own kingdom."

The moral is that change is fine, as long as you keep an eye out for those darned amphibolies!

READ UP

. . .

I ONCE READ THAT MORE THAN 50 PERCENT OF ALL
people who graduate from college never read another book with
the intention of learning something. It disturbed me immensely
because I had always been a reader but only for pleasure: I
avoided business books altogether. There is certainly nothing
wrong with reading for enjoyment, and I still do, but I enjoy
nothing more than learning something new. It struck me I was
missing out on a priceless opportunity to learn and get better at
what I do. Knowledge, after all, provides the ultimate advantage.
With so much information available, literally at my fingertips,
so easy to acquire and use, I considered it foolish and even lazy
of me not to take full advantage of it. As Peter Drucker warned,
"Knowledge has to be improved, challenged, and increased
constantly, or it vanishes."

The experience prompted me to up my game, so now I typically read a couple of books a week, or about 100 per year. Reading drives my passion to encourage others to read, and because I believe everyone should continue to learn, I've developed a penchant for giving books away. Friends and colleagues know, whenever they see me, they're sure to hear about a book or two that should be read, and I'm very likely to offer them a copy. Jack has a bookshelf in his den he calls the "Travis Library" and says he thinks it's strange I still cling to the belief that I can teach him a thing or two. He tells me, "You can give me all the books you want, but I'm still only going to read the ones I like."

Make no mistake: If you feel the ground moving under you, it's the tremors from the tsunami of change occurring in the marketing world. Customer conversation and big data analytics are revealing what people actually do. The social sciences are exposing the deeper reasons why people do what they do and why they respond to one brand versus another. Social marketing, online and mobile, is adding layers of complexity and opportunity we never imagined. Marketing, consumer research, and information technology are converging and becoming marketing science. Everything is changing so quickly, you can no longer stand still or, quite simply, you will be run over.

I've also heard the pace of change is making any five-year-old-or-more college curriculum hopelessly out of date. I hate to be the one to inform you, but your college degree has expired—or soon will. When I say *read* up, I really mean *keep* up! Unfortunately I can't give every one of you a book, and no one can read everything, except possibly my friend Tom Laforge, Global Director of Human & Cultural Insights at The Coca-Cola Company, as his job seems to include reading every interesting marketing and social science book ever published. Can you imagine actually getting paid to read and learn and explore new ideas and trends? I told Tom, "I always thought I had the best job in the world until I met you."

If you feel overwhelmed by the speed at which things are changing, there is a remedy: Read more, but read selectively. Realistically, we have jobs, families, friends, and distractions galore that keep even the best-intentioned learners from reading everything they might like to. I'm sure that's one reason why people always ask me for suggestions on what to read. Before you ask, here are my top recommendations: those I feel are the most interesting, informative, and provocative must-reads that will accelerate your learning curve. You will enjoy them. Once you have consumed this short list, you will be up-to-speed and well-informed, for the time being. More importantly, I'm convinced these books (and one magazine) will not only get you started but also whet your appetite for more. Please enjoy them!

1. The ultimate mind-altering read may be Dr. Timothy Wilson's *Strangers to Ourselves*. *If* you still cling to any belief that human beings are rational characters who know what they want, how they feel or what they think, this book will change your mind once and for all. Yes, it's a book about social psychology, but in case you haven't realized it by now, marketing is about social psychology.

2. Noble Prize–winner Daniel Kahneman is widely regarded as the most influential psychologist alive today and the father of behavioral economics. In *Thinking Fast and Slow*, he shares his extensive body of work in social psychology, cognitive science, and behavioral economics. This book will forever change

how you think about your customers and how you approach marketing.

3. *Herd* is Mark Earl's master treatise on how our human nature as social beings determines our beliefs and motivations. In the book, he makes a compelling case for how our social nature drives our cultural and consumption behaviors in ways we fail to fully comprehend. Marketers, you will view marketing in a whole new light after you read this book.

4. Sean Moffitt and Mike Dover's *Wikibrands* is a working manual that will quickly bring you up to speed on how brands come to life, or perish, in the modern social world. It's no different than when neighbors once talked with each other except there are a whole lot more neighbors talking over a whole new kind of backyard fence.

5. *The Invisible Gorilla*, by Christopher Chabris and Daniel Simons, is a book that will, in a good way, make you less sure of yourself. It's a very entertaining

and insightful read about how our intuitions and mental functions deceive us. Understanding how humans actually process information and make decisions is vital for business professionals to understand.

6. Daniel Pink's *A Whole New Mind* is a terrific primer on why creative thinking will rule the day in the future. With an urgent and thought-provoking perspective on the future that, by the way, arrived yesterday, it's a mind-altering but easy read.

7. Steven Johnson's *Mind Wide Open* will help you to learn out how our brains work and his *Where Good Ideas Come From* will help you understand how our brains spark great ideas. You will realize, as never before, exactly why creativity is linked to how our brains process information and experience. And you will probably get a few ideas of your own.

8. *Chip and Dan Heath's Made to Stick* and *Switch* are two books that provide basic concepts into how innovation, marketing and business processes are affected by how people think. Both books have plenty of case stories and practical examples of how you can use these new realizations about human nature.

9. Last but not least, I suggest you subscribe to the *Harvard Business Review.* The articles tend to be a bit behind the leading edge but several years ahead of current business thinking. One benefit of the *HBR* is each article includes a useful abstract so you can skim an entire issue to decide which articles, if any, you want to read fully. Even if you only skim the abstracts, you'll still have a good sense of the concepts your colleagues and customers will be discussing soon.

Thanks, Everyone...

● ● ●

I MENTIONED EARLIER THAT MY BOOK *EMOTIONAL Branding* is hopelessly and embarrassingly out-of-date. Though the principles haven't changed, the techniques and tools for creating brands are dramatically different from when that book was written. I'm so busy helping our clients, I neglected to pay attention to how dated the book had become. So, for all those who were kind enough to say they enjoyed the book, even though they must have noticed its many shortcomings, please accept my thanks for not bringing it up. You were very kind.

The entire staff at Brandtrust has contributed to this book in ways too numerous to mention. Our team does amazing work solving marketing problems and driving growth for many of the world's leading brands. I am inspired by their creativity, dedication, and passion for the work of revealing how people really think and make decisions. Many ideas shared in this book are the work of my teammates or were created out of the extraordinary work they do. In particular, Ed Jimenez created the beautiful book cover and text pages design; Valerie Hansen and Gillian Carter masterfully managed my schedule, the production milestones, and many of the marketing initiatives for the book; and Jill Van Nostran has done yeoman's work on the publicity. Thanks, guys.

I believe it's fitting to mention all the researchers, social scientists, and authors who are bringing to light the new realizations about *why* people do what they do and why feelings influence our every motivation and decision. These understandings will continue to profoundly influence how we build meaningful brands that truly meet their customer's needs. These revelations are sure to change how we think about the human element of almost everything in business, society, and life. We owe these thought leaders our respect and a debt of gratitude.

People ask if Harrison and I made Jack up, and we always respond, "No, he made himself up." Nevertheless, we thank him for his contributions. Without his unique perspective, it would not be possible to illustrate some of the ideas beyond anything but bullet points. Jack warns, "They're called bullet points for a reason." I think you know what he means.

Harrison is one of my favorite writers. We've worked together on many projects because I love working with him: He brings our ideas to life and he makes me laugh while doing it. He can always turn random piles of thoughts and notions into readable and engaging prose. And, his much better half, Monique, helps in so many ways with her critical eye and ear born of a long and fruitful career in the ad business. My endearing thanks to both of you.

Melissa Wilson and the team at Networlding have been indispensable helping us navigate the myriad publishing details of the book. I can't measure how much her perspective and experience has helped us with ideas and the discipline needed to stay on schedule and publish a respectable book. And Hallie Belt deserves special credit for a wonderful job on the final editing and proofreading.

My wife puts up with the disappointments, distractions, and demands for my time that writing a book extracts from our life. It should be expected to test any relationship, but she manages to help me overcome the challenges with patience, perseverance, and encouragement. Thank you, Donnita.